Ninja Foodi 2-Basket Air Fryer Cookbook for Beginners

2000 Days of Super Tasty and Healthy Air Fryer Recipes for Your Whole Family to Master Double Zone Air Fryer |Full Color Pictures

Vera V. Mull

Copyright© 2023 By Vera V. Mull
All Rights Reserved

This book is copyright protected. It is only for personal use. You cannot amend, distribute, sell, use, quote or paraphrase any part of the content within this book, without the consent of the author or publisher. Under no circumstances will any blame or legal responsibility be held against the publisher, or author, for any damages, reparation, or monetary loss due to the information contained within this book, either directly or indirectly.

Disclaimer Notice:

Please note the information contained within this document is for educational and entertainment purposes only. All effort has been executed to present accurate, up to date, reliable, complete information. No warranties of any kind are declared or implied. Readers acknowledge that the author is not engaged in the rendering of legal, financial, medical or professional advice. The content within this book has been derived from various sources. Please consult a licensed professional before attempting any techniques outlined in this book. By reading this document, the reader agrees that under no circumstances is the author responsible for any losses, direct or indirect, that are incurred as a result of the use of the information contained within this document, including, but not limited to, errors, omissions, or inaccuracies.

Contents

Introduction 1

CHAPTER 1   BREAKFAST 6

Avocado with Chorizo & Fried Eggs 7
Traditional Breakfast Hash 7
Smoked Salmon Bagel Toasts 8
Potato Scones with Smoked Bacon 8
Golden-Crisp Bacon, Sausage, and Egg Muffins 9
Breakfast Wraps with Scrambled Eggs and Bacon 9
Golden Syrup Flapjacks 10
Eggy Bread with Cinnamon-Spiced Topping 10
Breakfast Muffins with Blueberries 11
Easy Breakfast Crumpets 11
The Perfect Fry Up 12
Baked Eggs with Ham & Spinach 12

CHAPTER 2   POULTRY 13

Roast Chicken with Crackling 14
Massaman Curry Roast Turkey 14
Colourful Chicken Skewers 15
Chicken Cordon Bleu 15
Nutty Chicken Satay 16
Chicken Fajita Kebabs 16
Roast Duck Breast Salad 17
Chicken Kiev with Wild Garlic Butter 17
Turkey & Chorizo Jambalaya 18
Hunter's Chicken 18
Rustic Paella Mixta 19
Chicken Wings with Water Chestnuts 20
Queen's Coronation Chicken 20

Somerset Cider Chicken 21

Devilled Chicken 21

CHAPTER 3   MEAT 22

English Fry Up Skewers 23

Hand-Raised Pork Pies 23

Simple Pork Chops 24

Pork Shoulder with Bubble and Squeak 24

Classic Steak Pie 25

Beef Wellington Wontons 25

British Beef Jerky 26

Chorizo-Stuffed Pork Loin 26

Roast Pork Roulade 27

Homemade Pork Burgers with Chips 27

Pork Cutlets with Broccoli 28

Roast Beef with Pickled Red Cabbage 28

Steak Tips with Dried Tomato Pesto 29

Spiced Pork Medallions 29

CHAPTER 4   FISH & SEAFOOD 30

Blackened Shrimp 31

Salmon, Potato & Leek Traybake 31

Cod Fillets with Horseradish Sauce 32

Parmesan Crusted Tuna 32

Salmon with Capers 33

Crab Cakes with Garlic Mayo 33

Crab-Stuffed Avocado 34

Glazed Garlic Prawns 34

British Scampi 35

Garlic Lemon King Scallops 35

Fish Cakes with Asparagus 36

Fish Tacos 36

Halibut and Chickpea Salad 37

Fish & Chips Burger 37

CHAPTER 5   BEANS & GRAINS 38

Spicy Garlic Croutons 39
Paprika Roasted Chickpeas 39
Beans on Toast 40
Lentil and Coriander Burger with Chips 40
British Baked Beans 41
Griddle Scones with Clotted Cream 41
Staffordshire Oat Cake 42
Classic Cottage Loaf 42
Blackpool Milk Roll 43
Classic Bannock 43
Grandma's Stottie Cake 44
Sausage and Coriander Pilaf 44

CHAPTER 6   VEGETARIAN & VEGAN 45

Quorn and Mushroom Burgers 46
Veggie Tacos with Guacamole 46
Mushroom & Courgette Pilaf 47
Herb Cauliflower with Mushrooms 47
Mushrooms and Cherry Tomatoes on Toast 48
British-Style Gratin Dauphinois 48
Carrot & Oat Balls 49
Vegan "Chicken" with Asparagus 49
Lemony Falafel with Tahini Sauce 50
Spiced Cabbage Steaks 50
Cheese Aubergine Rolls 51
Herb Au Gratin Potatoes 51
Za'atar Potato Latkes 52
Mixed Air Fryer Vegetables 52

CHAPTER 7   APPETIZERS & SNACKS 53

Curried Corn on the Cob 54
Sweet Potato Chips 54
Classic British Faggots 55

Parmesan Okra Chips 55
Easy Cheesy Brussels Sprouts 56
Baked Spinach Dip 56
Sriracha Golden Cauliflower 57
Summer Squash Wedges 57
Squash Beignets 58
Worcestershire Chicken Wings 58
Colourful Vegetable Skewers 59

CHAPTER 8   DESSERTS 60
Bakewell Tart 61
Peach & Chocolate Galette 61
Chocolate Brownie Cake 62
Chocolate Doughnuts 62
Bread and Butter Pudding 63
Simple Scottish Cranachan 63
Dorset Apple Cake 64
Peach & Pistachio Frangipane 64

Introduction

Welcome to the Ninja Foodi 2-Basket Air Fryer Cookbook with my top 100, carefully crafted recipes! Whether you're new to cooking or a seasoned chef, you'll find something here to suit your preferences and enjoy air-fried food anytime, anywhere. If you're looking for a way to cook delicious fried foods and simplify your time in the kitchen, this cookbook might be your reliable kitchen ally!

First things first, the Ninja Foodi 2-Basket Air Fryer is not an ordinary air fryer. It is an Air Fryer with dual-zone cooking technology, offering a revolutionary approach to modern cooking! It has two independent drawers that allow us to cook two different foods at the same time! In other words, you can make a complete meal in one go; for instance, you do not have to wait for a main course to finish before cooking a side dish. Plus, there is the "SYNC" feature, so you can also sync the cooking times of both drawers, so everything is ready at the same time! Lovely! On the other hand, you can select "MATCH" to duplicate settings across both zones or to copy the settings from one drawer to the other, for a large batch of the same food. This means that you can use the Ninja 2-Basket Air Fryer to make crispy and tender food, saving time and energy while ensuring perfectly cooked meals. As a busy mom of two, coordinating cook times for different dishes is a difficult task for me. I love the fact that the Ninja Foodi 2-Basket Air Fryer can help me to multitask in the kitchen. Thanks to my Air Fryer, I can also make meal prepping a breeze. It offers me a head start on the busy week, giving healthier and better food options for the whole family. We have also managed to minimize buying takeaways and HFSS food.

There is a fact – people love fried food! It is hard to resist its aroma! We love that contrast between the crispy exterior and the tender interior! Did you know that the aroma of fried foods can trigger a so-called Pavlovian response, making you hungry and eager to eat immediately? Frying is deeply ingrained in the culinary traditions of many cultures worldwide. And last but not least, frying is a quick and convenient cooking method, isn't it? As you probably already know, HFSS food is not healthy, contributing to health issues such as cardiovascular problems, obesity, and diabetes. With the Ninja Foodi 2-Basket Air Fryer, we can balance indulgence with health, using up to 75% less fat than traditional cooking methods!

How to Clean the Ninja Foodi 2-Basket Air Fryer?
Your Ninja Foodi 2-Basket Air Fryer will accumulate food particles and smells over time, so regular cleaning is essential.
- Cleaning the Exterior. Simply wipe it down with damp towels. For stubborn stains, you can use a mild washing-up liquid. Do not use harsh chemicals and

always dry the exterior before storing your Ninja Foodi 2-Basket Air Fryer. Do not forget to wipe the control panel with a slightly damp kitchen towel that is not dripping.
- Cleaning the Heating Elements. Make sure the unit is unplugged and completely cool before cleaning. Make sure to remove any loose debris using a soft towel. Submerging the heating elements in the water is a big no-no!
- Cleaning the Cooking Elements. Drawers and crisper plates of your Ninja Foodi come into direct contact with your food, so it's crucial to keep them in good condition. Be cautious not to scratch any non-stick surfaces. Remove any food debris and soak them in warm soapy water for about 10 minutes. Keep in mind that abrasive cleaners with small mineral particles can damage the finish. Use a sponge to scrub away the residue and be cautious not to scratch any non-stick surfaces. It is essential to rinse the components thoroughly and dry them completely before storing them.

I wanted to share with you some extra tips to keep your Ninja Foodi 2-Basket Air Fryer in top condition:
- Check the user manual periodically to keep the Ninja Foodi 2-Basket Air Fryer in top shape. Following safety guidelines and maintaining the appliance properly will help ensure a safe and enjoyable cooking experience!
- Avoid using metal items (spatulas, spoons, etc.) that can scratch the non-stick surface.
- Clean the cooking basket after each use to prevent the buildup of hardened food residues. This practice will not only ensure the longevity of your machine but also keep your food tasting amazing!
- If there are stubborn stains or residue, use a mixture of vinegar and water and gently wipe the components. A mixture of water and bicarbonate of soda is also a good idea for easy cleaning!

To Use or Not to Use: Potential Risks of your Ninja Foodi 2-Basket Air Fryer

Electric Shock. To minimise the risk of electric shock, always ensure that the machine is properly plugged in; also, the power cord should be in good condition. While air fryers are generally safe, avoid handling the appliance with wet hands.

Fire Hazard. There is a risk of fire if used improperly. Do not use flammable materials with your Air Fryer. Make sure to check recommended cooking times and temperatures to prevent overheating. Avoid overloading the cooking basket and follow the recommended quantity to help your machine work properly.

Using your Ninja Foodi 2-Basket Air Fryer for purposes other than its intended function can pose risks. Use it only for its designated cooking functions.

Hot Surfaces. There are hot components during operation. Use oven mitts when touching hot cooking baskets, drawers, and crisper plates. Allow it to cool before cleaning and storing.

Children and Pets. Keep your machine out of reach of children and pets to prevent accidental injuries. To mitigate potential risks, it's essential to adhere to the user manual that comes with your machine.

Tips and Tricks for the Ninja Foodi 2-Basket Air Fryer

Successful air fryer preheating. Yes, it is true, preheating works wonders for your air-fried food. It ensures the specific crispy exterior and satisfying crunch of fried foods! The amount of preheating time required will vary based on the model of your Air Fryer. In general, preheating will reduce your total cooking time because moisture will be removed immediately from the food surface. Some foods do not require preheating, but if you are not sure – preheat; it can't hurt!

Stirring and tossing the ingredients. Shake the cooking basket during cooking. It helps distribute the heat evenly and cook your food properly.

SINC and MATCH functions. You can sync your dishes to finish at the same time or use the match cook function to copy the settings across both zones. Simply press the "MATCH" cook button and the settings from one basket will be applied to the other.

Use cooking oil in moderation. Use a mister or pastry brush to apply a thin layer of good-quality oil and your health and waistline will thank you. Using too much oil can make your food greasy and unhealthy.

Embrace layering techniques. Pay attention to the cooking times of different items. Start with the longer cooking items and add the quicker ones later.

Spice it up! Do not be shy with herbs, spices, and rubs; they will enhance the flavour of your air-fried foods. I like to toss the ingredients with the seasonings in a mixing bowl (or a bag) before placing them in the cooking basket.

Don't overcrowd the cooking basket. How much food can we cook in the Ninja Foodi 2-Basket Air Fryer? Yes, I know, it is tempting to pile it all in, but every item needs some breathing room. The amount of food you can cook in the Air Fryer depends on the size of the appliance. Most models can accommodate up to 6-8 servings of food at a time.

Get adventurous with your Ninja Air Fryer! Try different cuisines, tweak temperatures, and experiment with seasonings. The Ninja Foodi 2-Basket Air Fryer is versatile and can cook a wide variety of foods. Don't be afraid to experiment with different foods and recipes to find what works best for you.

Clean as you go! Clean your Air Fryer after each use to keep it in top shape. The removable parts are usually dishwasher-safe, so it won't be a problem at all!

Frequently Asked Questions

1. Can I use tin foil and baking parchment in my Ninja Foodi 2-Basket Air Fryer?

Yes, you can use these kitchen products, but it's important to avoid blocking the airflow or covering the entire basket with foil; in other words, it can prevent the food from cooking evenly.

2. Is the Ninja Foodi 2-Basket Air Fryer safe to use?

Yes, it is generally safe to use like most of the Air Fryers on the market. But it's crucial to follow the manufacturer's guidelines and keep it away from children, pets, and flammable materials!

3. What type of oil can be used in the Ninja Foodi 2-Basket Air Fryer?

Although air frying doesn't require as much oil as traditional frying, you'll still need to use some oil for crunchy results. Use high-quality olive oil, grapeseed oil, peanut oil, or sesame oil. These oils have a high smoke point and can withstand high temperatures.

4. What types of food can I cook in the Ninja Foodi 2-Basket Air Fryer?

You can cook a wide variety of fried foods, including fish, chips, wings, vegetables, doughnuts, and even desserts. Try air-frying frozen snacks such as onion rings, pastries, and mini quiches. You can roast vegetables and toast nuts to perfection in your Air Fryer. Enjoy the crispiness and deliciousness of wonton wrappers and spring rolls without the deep-frying mess.

You can also cook frozen foods directly. You do not need to defrost your food before cooking in the Air Fryer. For instance, if you're cooking frozen chips, you may need to preheat the air fryer to 200°C.

5. What can I not cook in the Ninja Foodi 2-Basket Air Fryer

You cannot cook watery foods such as soups and stews. Foods with wet batter might not work well in the Ninja Foodi 2-Basket Air Fryer since the batter can drip through the basket and create a mess. Avoid using excessive oil and marinades; it can lead to smoking and burning. Further, you cannot cook large roasts or a whole turkey due to the capacity of the cooking basket. While you can cook dishes with cheese, make sure you use baking dishes to avoid melting and smoking. Last but not least, foods that release a lot of moisture during cooking, such as very juicy fruits and vegetables, might not get the desired texture in the Ninja Foodi 2-Basket Zone Air Fryer.

6. What type of accessories can I use in my Ninja Foodi 2-Basket Air Fryer

This kitchen wizard usually comes with a variety of accessories, such as a crisper plate and a multi-layer rack. In general, you can use oven-safe tins, trays, silicone cases, and other bakeare. Use a silicone-tipped or wooden spatula to keep the cooking basket in good condition.

7. Why is the internal temperature of my food important?

When the cooking cycle is complete, check the internal temperature of the food to ensure it has reached a safe temperature (this is particularly important for meat products).

8. Can I dehydrate food in my Ninja Foodi 2-Basket Air Fryer?

You can use the "DEHIDRATE" function to prepare homemade dried fruits, vegetables, and other foods. Arrange the slices on the cooking tray, making sure they don't overlap; then, adjust the temperature and time according to the air fryer's manual.

9. Can I bake in my Ninja Foodi 2-Basket Air Fryer?

Yes, it can be used for baking. It is capable of baking a variety of items, including casseroles, muffins, and even cakes. Plus, you can air-broil their surfaces for golden, crispy results. Adjust the temperature and cooking time as needed.

10. Can I use butter or other fats in my Ninja Foodi 2-Basket Air Fryer?

While you can use a small amount of butter or animal fats, such as lard, it's important to avoid excessive amounts, as this machine is designed to reduce oil usage. If you are trying to use too much fat or butter, it can result in smoke and affect the cooking process.

As you flip through the pages of this recipe collection, you'll discover 100 amazing, hand-picked recipes that showcase the capabilities of the Ninja Air Fryer. This means that this book is more than just a collection of recipes; it's your guide to unlocking the incredible potential of your new kitchen device. Are you ready to explore new ways to use your Air Fryer? I know I am ready! So, what are you waiting for? I'm so excited to share with you my best tips for air frying. Let's get cooking!

CHAPTER 1
BREAKFAST

Avocado with Chorizo & Fried Eggs

Prep time: 10 minutes
Cook time: 15 minutes
Serves 4

Per Serving:
Calories: 490
Fat: 33.2g
Carbs: 25.8g
Fibre: 8g
Protein: 20.7g

- 2 large avocados, pitted and cut in half
- 4 medium eggs
- 1 small chilli pepper, chopped
- 160g chorizo, sliced into chunks
- 1 small pack of coriander, chopped
- Sea salt and ground black pepper, to taste
- 4 thick-cut slices of wholemeal bread

Instructions
1. Cut the avocados in half and carefully remove the pits. Scoop out about 2 tablespoons of avocado flesh from the centre of each half; reserve.
2. Beat the eggs with the reserved avocado flesh and chilli pepper. Spoon the mixture into each avocado half.
3. Season to taste and add avocado halves to the zone 1 drawer and chorizo to the zone 2 drawer.
4. Select zone 1 and pair it with "BAKE" at 190°C for 15 minutes. Select zone 2 and pair it with "AIR FRY" at 180°C for 12 minutes. Select "SYNC" followed by the "START/STOP" button.
5. When zone 2 time reaches 6 minutes, toss the chorizo to ensure even browning; then, reinsert the drawer to resume cooking.
6. Cook until the chorizo becomes crisp. Add the chorizo to the avocado halves and serve with the wholemeal bread.

Enjoy!

Traditional Breakfast Hash

Prep time: 10 minutes
Cook time: 25 minutes
Serves 4

Per Serving:
Calories: 330
Fat: 15.5g
Carbs: 35.4g
Fibre: 4.7g
Protein: 13.5g

- 600g potatoes
- 1 medium onion, sliced
- 1 bell pepper, sliced (any colour)
- 150g cherry tomatoes, halved
- 1 tsp smoked paprika
- Sea salt and ground black pepper, to taste
- 4 rashers bacon, chopped
- 4 large eggs

Instructions
1. Peel the potatoes and cut them into a bowl.
2. Add the vegetables and spices, and stir to ensure they are evenly coated. Place the seasoned vegetables in the zone 1 and 2 drawers.
3. Select zone 1 and pair it with "BAKE" at 200°C for 15 minutes. Select "MATCH" followed by the "START/STOP" button.
4. Make sure to stir the vegetables halfway through and cook until the potatoes are cooked through.
5. Remove the cooking basket and top your vegetables with bacon.
6. Using a spoon, create four wells in the vegetable mixture. Carefully crack an egg into each well, ensuring the yolk stays intact.
7. Place the cooking basket back into your Ninja Air Fryer; cook at 180°C for an additional 10 minutes or until the eggs are set.

Bon appétit!

Smoked Salmon Bagel Toasts

Prep time: 10 minutes
Cook time: 6 minutes
Serves 4

Per Serving:
Calories: 516
Fat: 22.1g
Carbs: 54g
Fibre: 1.7g
Protein: 24.5g

- 4 whole-grain bagels, split
- 1 tsp olive oil
- 200g tubs cream cheese
- 2 (120g) packs smoked salmon trimmings
- Sea salt and ground black pepper, to taste
- 1 tbsp capers, drained
- 1 small lemon, cut into slices

Instructions
1. Brush the bagel halves with olive oil on both sides.
2. Assemble bagels: Spread a generous layer of cream cheese on each bagel half. Add smoked salmon, salt, black pepper, and capers.
3. Place the bagel halves in the zone 1 and zone 2 drawers.
4. Select zone 1 and pair it with "BAKE" at 190°C for 6 minutes. Select "MATCH" followed by the "START/STOP" button.
5. Garnish with lemon slices and serve immediately while the bagels are still warm. Enjoy!

Potato Scones with Smoked Bacon

Prep time: 10 minutes
Cook time: 17 minutes
Serves 4

Per Serving:
Calories: 63
Fat: 26.4g
Carbs: 77.4g
Fibre: 5.7g
Protein: 21.2g

- 2 medium potatoes, cut into cubes
- 200g plain flour
- Sea salt and ground black pepper, to taste
- 20g dill, roughly chopped
- 1 tsp baking powder
- 60g butter, melted
- 5 tbsp milk, plus more for brushing
- 2 medium eggs, beaten
- 4 (25g) rashers smoked bacon
- A few drizzles of honey

Instructions
1. Cook the potatoes in plenty of salted simmering water until cooked through. Drain and mash.
2. Sift the flour, spices, and baking powder into a bowl. Next, stir in the melted butter, milk, and eggs; mix into a sticky dough.
3. Spoon dollops of the dough into two lightly oiled baking tins. Glaze the tops of your scones with a little milk.
4. Select zone 1 and pair it with "BAKE" at 200°C for 10 minutes. Select "MATCH" followed by the "START/STOP" button.
5. At the halfway point, turn your scones over to promote even cooking; reinsert the drawers to resume cooking. Reserve.
6. Add bacon to the cooking basket and drizzle each piece with a drizzle of honey. Select zone 1 and pair it with "AIR FRY" at 180°C for 7 minutes. Select "MATCH" followed by the "START/STOP" button.
7. Serve warm scones with crisp, sticky bacon on the side.

Bon appétit!

Golden-Crisp Bacon, Sausage, and Egg Muffins

Prep time: 10 minutes
Cook time: 13 minutes
Serves 8

Per Serving:
Calories: 365
Fat: 31g
Carbs: 4.6g
Fibre: 0g
Protein: 14.1g

- 6 large eggs, lightly beaten
- 200g cream cheese
- 200g sausage, crumbled
- 2 rashers bacon, chopped
- 1 tbsp butter, room temperature
- 1 tbsp golden syrup
- 1/2 tsp cayenne pepper
- Sea salt and ground black pepper, to taste

Instructions

1. Lightly butter 8 muffin cases.
2. In a mixing bowl, thoroughly combine all the ingredients.
3. Spoon the mixture into the prepared muffin cases. Place 4 muffin cases in each drawer.
4. Select zone 1 and pair it with "BAKE" at 180°C for 13 minutes or until cooked through. Select "MATCH" followed by the "START/STOP" button.
5. Cool in the cases for 10 minutes; then lift out onto a wire rack to finish cooling.

Bon appétit!

Breakfast Wraps with Scrambled Eggs and Bacon

Prep time: 10 minutes
Cook time: 15 minutes
Serves 4

Per Serving:
Calories: 512
Fat: 28.8g
Carbs: 41.1g
Fibre: 2.6g
Protein: 20.9g

- 8 medium eggs
- 4 tbsp single cream
- 1 tbsp olive oil
- A pinch of cayenne pepper
- 1 tsp English mustard powder
- 4 (25g) rashers bacon
- Sea salt and ground black pepper, to taste
- 1 large tomato, diced
- 4 large tortillas

Instructions

1. Remove a crisper plate from the zone 1 drawer of your Ninja Air Fryer. Preheat your Ninja Air Fryer to 180°C for 5 minutes.
2. Beat the eggs with single cream, oil and cayenne pepper; spoon the mixture into a baking tin. Lower the baking tin into the zone 1 drawer. Add the bacon to the zone 2 drawer (with a crisper plate inside).
3. Select zone 1 and pair it with "BAKE" at 180°C for 10 minutes. Select zone 2 and pair it with "AIR FRY" at 190°C for 10 minutes. Select "SYNC" followed by the "START/STOP" button.
4. When zone 2 time reaches 5 minutes, stir the eggs with a wooden spoon, lifting and folding them over from the bottom of the tin; then, reinsert the drawer to resume cooking.
5. Assemble your tortillas with scrambled eggs, bacon, and tomato; add salt, pepper and mustard.
6. Roll them up to make wraps and lower them into the cooking basket. Use "REHEAT" mode to bake your wraps at 180°C for 5 minutes, until warmed through. Enjoy!

Golden Syrup Flapjacks

Prep time: 10 minutes
Cook time: 20 minutes
Serves 8

Per Serving:
Calories: 333
Fat: 15.2g
Carbs: 46.2g
Fibre: 5.5g
Protein: 6.5g

- 300g old-fashioned rolled oats
- 100g coconut oil, room temperature
- 150g golden syrup
- A pinch of sea salt
- 1 tsp cinnamon powder
- 2 medium overripe pears, peeled, cored and diced

Instructions
1. Brush two baking tins with nonstick cooking spray. Mix all the ingredients in your food processor.
2. Lightly butter two baking tins and add the mixture; press into the corners with a spatula so the mixture is flat and score into squares.
3. Place one baking tin in each drawer.
4. Select zone 1 and pair it with "BAKE" at 180°C for 20 minutes. Select "MATCH" followed by the "START/STOP" button. Bake until golden brown.
5. Leave your Flapjacks to cool completely in the tins.

Bon appétit!

Eggy Bread with Cinnamon-Spiced Topping

Prep time: 10 minutes
Cook time: 15 minutes
Serves 4

Per Serving:
Calories: 248
Fat: 11.9g
Carbs: 29.3g
Fibre: 5g
Protein: 6.6g

- 2 large eggs
- 4 tbsp double cream
- 4 thick slices of day-old brioche
- 2 tbsp butter, room temperature
- 50g golden caster sugar
- 20g ground cinnamon

Instructions
1. Lightly beat the eggs in a shallow bowl along with double cream.
2. Dip bread slices in the custard mixture until they are well coated on all sides.
3. Lower eggy bread into the drawers and brush them with the butter.
4. Select zone 1 and pair it with "AIR FRYER" at 180°C for 15 minutes. Select "MATCH" followed by the "START/STOP" button.
5. In the meantime, mix the sugar with cinnamon to make the topping. Spread the topping over each eggy bread slice and serve warm.

Bon appétit!

Breakfast Muffins with Blueberries

Prep time: 10 minutes
Cook time: 15 minutes
Serves 9

Per Serving:
Calories: 256
Fat: 6.8g
Carbs: 44.8g
Fibre: 3.2g
Protein: 5.1g

- 120g rolled oats
- 200g plain flour
- 1 tsp bicarbonate of soda
- 1 tsp baking powder
- A pinch of sea salt
- A pinch of grated nutmeg
- 1/2 tsp ground cinnamon
- 300g banana, mashed
- 100g golden syrup
- 50g grapeseed oil
- 1 small orange, juiced
- 100g blueberries

Instructions
1. Remove a crisper plate from your Ninja Air Fryer. Spray 9 muffin cases with nonstick oil.
2. In a mixing bowl, thoroughly combine all the dry ingredients. Then, slowly and gradually, stir in the liquid ingredients; mix until everything is well incorporated.
3. Fold in the blueberries. Spoon the batter into the prepared muffin cases and lower them into the cooking basket.
4. Select zone 1 and pair it with "BAKE" at 160°C for 15 minutes. Select "MATCH" followed by the "START/STOP" button.
5. Bake until a cocktail stick inserted into the centre comes out clean.
6. Keep for up to 4 days in an airtight container. You can pop your muffins in the Ninja Air Fryer to reheat them and freshen them up. Enjoy!

Easy Breakfast Crumpets

Prep time: 10 minutes
Cook time: 6 minutes
Serves 4

Per Serving:
Calories: 450
Fat: 30.1g
Carbs: 22.4g
Fibre: 1.7g
Protein: 20.5g

- 4 large crumpets
- 1 tbsp butter, melted
- 4 medium eggs
- 100g cheddar cheese, shredded
- 4 (30g) rashers back bacon
- 4 tbsp passata
- Sea salt and cayenne pepper, to taste

Instructions
1. Brush your crumpets with the melted butter on both sides.
2. Beat the eggs with cheese.
3. Assemble crumpets: Spread passata on each crumpet. Add the filling and bacon; lower them into the cooking basket.
4. Select zone 1 and pair it with "BAKE" at 190°C for 6 minutes. Select "MATCH" followed by the "START/STOP" button.

Bon appétit!

The Perfect Fry Up

Prep time: 10 minutes
Cook time: 27 minutes
Serves 4

Per Serving:
Calories: 603
Fat: 50g
Carbs: 11.5g
Fibre: 1.4g
Protein: 28.1g

- 400g button mushrooms, halved
- 1 tsp cayenne pepper
- Sea salt and ground black pepper, to taste
- 4 pork sausages, smoked
- 4 rashers smoked bacon
- 4 small eggs
- 100g canned cannellini beans, drained and rinsed
- 4 slices of black and white pudding (optional)

Instructions
1. Toss the mushrooms with cayenne pepper, salt, and black pepper. Insert a crisper plate in both drawers. Spray the plates with nonstick cooking oil.
2. Add the sausages to the zone 1 drawer; add the mushrooms and bacon to the zone 2 drawer.
3. Select zone 1 and pair it with "AIR FRY" at 200°C for 15 minutes. Select zone 2 and pair it with "AIR FRY" at 180°C for 10 minutes. Select "SYNC" followed by the "START/STOP" button.
4. Crack the eggs in the lightly oiled muffin cases. Place muffin cases in the cooking basket and air fry them at 180°C for 12 minutes.
5. Place all ingredients on serving plates and serve with cannellini beans and pudding. Devour!

Baked Eggs with Ham & Spinach

Prep time: 10 minutes
Cook time: 14 minutes
Serves 6

Per Serving:
Calories: 190
Fat: 10.1g
Carbs: 8.5g
Fibre: 2.4g
Protein: 17.5g

- 100g double cream
- 300g ham, sliced
- 900g ripe vine tomatoes
- 200g baby spinach
- 1 tsp paprika
- Sea salt and ground black pepper, to taste
- 6 large eggs

Instructions
1. Remove a crisper plate from your Ninja Air Fryer.
2. In a mixing bowl, thoroughly combine all the ingredients, except the eggs.
3. Divide the mixture between two lightly greased baking tins.
4. Make six gaps between the tomatoes and ham.
5. Now, break an egg into each gap. Sprinkle the eggs with some extra salt and pepper.
6. Cover the tins with a sheet of foil and lower them into the cooking basket.
7. Select zone 1 and pair it with "BAKE" at 180°C for 14 minutes. Select "MATCH" followed by the "START/STOP" button.

Bon appétit!

CHAPTER 2
POULTRY

Roast Chicken with Crackling

Prep time: 10 minutes
Cook time: 35 minutes
Serves 6

Per Serving:
Calories: 407
Fat: 12.1g
Carbs: 1.8g
Fibre: 0.4g
Protein: 68.1g

- 2kg whole chicken, cut into two pieces, boneless
- 2 garlic cloves
- 1 small bunch thyme, chopped
- 1 tsp smoked paprika, or to taste
- Sea salt and ground black pepper, to taste
- 1 lemon, juiced
- 25g butter, softened

Instructions
1. Pat the chicken dry using tea towels.
2. Crush the garlic and spices using a pestle and mortar. Rub the chicken with the butter lemon juice, and spice mix.
3. Place the prepared chicken in the cooking basket, skin-side down.
4. Select zone 1 and pair it with "AIR FRY" at 190°C for 35 minutes. Select "MATCH" followed by the "START/STOP" button.
5. When zone 1 time reaches 20 minutes, turn them over, and reinsert the drawer to continue cooking.

Bon appétit!

Massaman Curry Roast Turkey

Prep time: 5 minutes
Cook time: 1 hour
Serves 4

Per Serving:
Calories: 470
Fat: 15.8g
Carbs: 18.5g
Fibre: 0.9g
Protein: 71g

- 1.2 kg turkey breasts, skin-on, boneless, cut into two pieces
- 40g butter, at room temperature
- 20ml lime juice
- 1 packet of massaman curry paste
- 2 garlic cloves, crushed
- Sea salt and ground black pepper, to taste

Instructions
1. Insert crisper plates in both drawers. Spray the crisper plates with nonstick cooking oil.
2. Pat turkey breasts dry with tea towels. Mix the butter with the remaining ingredients. Rub turkey all over with the butter mixture.
3. Select zone 1 and pair it with "ROAST" at 200°C for 1 hour. Select "MATCH" to duplicate settings across both zones. Press the "START/STOP" button.
4. At the halfway point, turn the turkey breasts over and reinsert the drawers to resume cooking.

Bon appétit!

Colourful Chicken Skewers

Prep time: 10 minutes
Cook time: 20 minutes
Serves 5

Per Serving:
Calories: 460
Fat: 15.6g
Carbs: 2.8g
Fibre: 0.9g
Protein: 72.2g

- 1.5 kg chicken breasts, cut into bite-sized pieces
- 100g bacon lardons
- 100h cherry tomatoes
- 1 large bell pepper, deseeded and sliced
- 1 small zucchini, sliced
- 1 tbsp olive oil
- 1 tsp garlic powder
- Sea salt and ground black pepper, to taste

Instructions
1. If you are using wooden skewers, make sure to soak them for about 1 hour; otherwise, they will burn in your air fryer.
2. Pat the chicken dry using tea towels; toss the chicken along with the other ingredients in a large bowl.
3. Thread the chicken, bacon, and vegetables onto the soaked wooden (or metal) skewers.
4. Select zone 1 and pair it with "AIR FRY" at 190°C for 20 minutes. Select "MATCH" to duplicate settings across both zones. Press the "START/STOP" button.
5. When zone 1 time reaches 10 minutes, turn the skewers over and then, reinsert the drawers to continue cooking.

Bon appétit!

Chicken Cordon Bleu

Prep time: 10 minutes
Cook time: 30 minutes
Serves 4

Per Serving:
Calories: 750
Fat: 30.2g
Carbs: 56.2g
Fibre: 2.7g
Protein: 58.1g

- 800g chicken breasts, pounded out to 1cm thick
- 100g cheddar cheese
- 1 tsp salt
- 1 tsp paprika
- 400g plain flour
- 1 tsp freshly ground black pepper
- 2 eggs
- 60g bacon lardons
- 200g biscuit crumbs

Instructions
1. Take a piece of chicken and place the bacon and cheese in the middle. Roll up the chicken breasts tightly and use cocktail sticks to secure them. Repeat for all the ingredients.
2. Insert crisper plates in both drawers. Spray the crisper plates with nonstick cooking oil.
3. Place the prepared chicken rolls in both drawers.
4. Select zone 1 and pair it with "AIR FRY" at 190°C for 20 minutes. Select "MATCH" to duplicate settings across both zones. Press the "START/STOP" button.
5. At the halfway point, flip the chicken breasts with silicone-tipped tongs to promote even browning. Reinsert drawers to resume cooking.
6. Combine the flour, biscuit crumbs, and spices on a large plate. Beat the eggs in a wide, shallow bowl.
7. Place the chicken rolls in the beaten egg and then coat them with the breading mixture; make sure to coat them on all sides.
8. Select zone 1 and pair it with "BAKE" at 190°C for 10 minutes. Select "MATCH" to duplicate settings across both zones. Press the "START/STOP" button.
9. Serve warm and enjoy!

Nutty Chicken Satay

Prep time: 1 hour
Cook time: 20 minutes
Serves 4

Per Serving:
Calories: 346
Fat: 12.5g
Carbs: 13.3g
Fibre: 1.3g
Protein: 43.5g

- 800g chicken fillets, sliced
- Marinade:
- 1 tsp olive oil
- 2 tbsp fresh lime juice
- 1 tbsp Sriracha sauce
- 20g ground ginger
- Sauce:
- 150ml chicken broth, low sodium
- 2 tbsp fish sauce
- 1 tbsp honey
- 2 spring onions, thinly sliced
- 1 tbsp soy sauce
- 2 cloves garlic, minced
- 1 tbsp peanut oil
- 2 tbsp creamy peanut butter

Instructions
1. Mix all the marinade ingredients in a ceramic bowl. Add the chicken to the bowl and let it marinate for about 1 hour.
2. Spray the crisper plates with nonstick cooking oil. Then thread the chicken onto skewers.
3. Select zone 1 and pair it with "AIR FRY" at 190°C for 20 minutes. Select "MATCH" to duplicate settings across both zones. Press the "START/STOP" button.
4. When zone 1 time reaches 10 minutes, turn the skewers over and then, reinsert the drawers to continue cooking.
5. Meanwhile, whisk all the sauce ingredients. Serve warm satay with peanut sauce on the side. Enjoy!

Chicken Fajita Kebabs

Prep time: 10 minutes
Cook time: 25 minutes
Serves 4

Per Serving:
Calories: 305
Fat: 7.4g
Carbs: 28g
Fibre: 3.7g
Protein: 29.7g

- 500g chicken breasts, sliced
- 2 medium bell peppers, deseeded and halved
- 2 medium shallots, peeled and cut into wedges • 2 tsp olive oil
- 1 lime, juiced
- 1 tsp dried Mexican oregano
- Sea salt and freshly ground black pepper, to taste
- Tabasco, to taste
- 4 medium corn tortillas

Instructions
1. Insert crisper plates in both drawers. Spray the crisper plates with nonstick cooking oil.
2. Toss the chicken, peppers, and shallots with olive oil, lime juice, spices, and Tabasco.
3. Place the chicken in the zone 1 drawer; place the peppers and shallots in the zone 2 drawer.
4. Select zone 1 and pair it with "AIR FRY" at 190°C for 20 minutes. Select zone 2 and pair it with "ROAST" at 190°C for 15 minutes. Select "SYNC" followed by the "START/STOP" button.
5. Shake the basket once or twice to promote even cooking. Reinsert the drawers to resume cooking.
6. Thread the chicken and vegetables onto the soaked wooden (or metal) skewers.
7. Add tortillas to both drawers. Select "REHEAT" at 170°C for 5 minutes. Serve immediately with kebabs and enjoy!

Roast Duck Breast Salad

Prep time: 35 minutes
Cook time: 20 minutes
Serves 4

Per Serving:
Calories: 303
Fat: 12.7g
Carbs: 14.2g
Fibre: 2.5g
Protein: 32.6g

- 600g duck breasts, boneless and cut into 2 pieces
- 1 tbsp sesame oil
- 2 tbsp soy sauce
- 2 tbsp lime juice
- Sea salt and ground black pepper, to taste
- 4 medium bell peppers, deseeded and halved
- 2 tsp extra-virgin olive oil
- 1 medium tomato, diced
- 1 small shallot, sliced
- 1 small cucumber, sliced

Instructions
1. Pat the duck breasts dry with tea towels.
2. In a mixing bowl, toss the duck breasts with the sesame oil, soy sauce, lime juice, salt, and pepper; let it marinate for about 30 minutes in your fridge.
3. Add the duck to the zone 1 drawer and pepper halves to the zone 2 drawer. Brush the peppers and meat with olive oil.
4. Select zone 1 and pair it with "ROAST" at 195°C for 20 minutes. Select zone 2 and pair it with "ROAST" at 200°C for 15 minutes. Select "SYNC" followed by the "START/STOP" button.
5. At the half point, turn your ingredients over to promote even cooking. Reinsert drawers to resume cooking.
6. Cut duck breasts into strips and add them to a salad bowl; add the roasted peppers along with the other ingredients; toss to combine.

Bon appétit!

Chicken Kiev with Wild Garlic Butter

Prep time: 10 minutes
Cook time: 30 minutes
Serves 4

Per Serving:
Calories: 603
Fat: 36.2g
Carbs: 21.4g
Fibre: 2.3g
Protein: 48.6g

- 4 (200g each) chicken fillets
- Sea salt and ground black pepper, to taste
- 1 tbsp olive oil, room temperature
- 100g dried breadcrumbs
- 100g parmesan, preferably freshly grated
- Wild Garlic Butter:
- 4 wild garlic stalks, crushed
- 2 tbsp coriander, finely chopped
- 2 tbsp lemon juice
- 100g butter, softened

Instructions
1. Rub the chicken with salt, black pepper, and olive oil. Then, roll the chicken over the breadcrumbs and parmesan.
2. Insert crisper plates in both drawers. Spray the crisper plates with nonstick cooking oil.
3. Place the chicken breasts in both drawers.
4. Select zone 1 and pair it with "AIR FRY" at 190°C for 30 minutes. Select "MATCH" to duplicate settings across both zones. Press the "START/STOP" button.
5. At the halfway point, flip the chicken breasts with silicone-tipped tongs to promote even browning. Reinsert drawers to resume cooking.
6. Meanwhile, place all the wild garlic butter ingredients in a bowl. Mash the ingredients with a fork until well combined; tightly wrap and chill until firm and ready to serve.
7. Serve kievs topped with wild garlic butter and enjoy!

Turkey & Chorizo Jambalaya

Prep time: 5 minutes
Cook time: 20 minutes
Serves 6

Per Serving:
Calories: 592
Fat: 38.7g
Carbs: 38.1g
Fibre: 3.1g
Protein: 21.6g

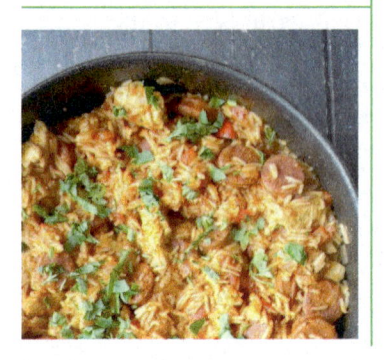

- 250g long grain rice
- 300g leftover turkey, diced
- 200g chorizo, diced
- 1 tbsp olive oil
- 1 large onion, sliced
- 2 garlic cloves, chopped
- 1 tsp ground turmeric
- 1/2 tsp garam masala
- 400g can passata
- 2 tsp vegetable bouillon powder

Instructions
1. Lightly grease two baking tins with cooking oil.
2. Cook the rice according to the pack instructions or until tender; fluff the rice with a fork and divide it between the prepared tins.
3. Divide the other ingredients between the prepared tins. Lower the tins into both drawers.
4. Select zone 1 and pair it with "AIR FRY" at 185°C for 20 minutes. Select "MATCH" to duplicate settings across both zones. Press the "START/STOP" button.
5. When zone 1 time reaches 10 minutes, gently stir the ingredients to ensure even cooking. Reinsert the drawers to continue cooking. Enjoy!

Hunter's Chicken

Prep time: 5 minutes
Cook time: 22 minutes
Serves 4

Per Serving:
Calories: 506
Fat: 23.7g
Carbs: 23.8g
Fibre: 3.1g
Protein: 47.6g

- 4 skinless chicken legs, boneless
- 4 (30g) rashers streaky bacon
- 1 tbsp vegetable oil, plus extra for the tray
- 50ml sticky BBQ sauce
- British Mash:
- 500g potatoes, peeled and diced (Dutch Cream, Desiree, or Maris Piper)
- 50ml milk
- 2 tbsp cream cheese

Instructions
1. Place the chicken legs on the tray and then, wrap a slice of bacon around each. Place them in the zone 1 drawer.
2. Toss the potatoes with 1 tablespoon of oil and arrange them in the zone 2 drawer.
3. Select zone 1 and pair it with "AIR FRY" at 200°C for 20 minutes. Select zone 2 and pair it with "ROAST" at 190°C for 22 minutes. Select "SYNC" followed by the "START/STOP" button.
4. When zone 1 time reaches 10 minutes, shake the drawer to ensure even cooking; baste the chicken with sticky BBQ sauce and reinsert the drawer to continue cooking.
5. When zone 2 time reaches 11 minutes, shake the drawer to ensure even cooking; reinsert drawers to continue cooking.
6. Mash roasted potatoes with milk and cream cheese. Serve warm chicken with British mash on the side.

Bon appétit!

Rustic Paella Mixta

Prep time: 10 minutes
Cook time: 31 minutes
Serves 6

Per Serving:
Calories: 660
Fat: 29.7g
Carbs: 53.8g
Fibre: 4.3g
Protein: 44.6g

- 250g prawns, peeled, tails-on
- 2 bell peppers, deseeded and sliced
- 3 tbsp olive oil
- Sea salt and Spanish paprika, to taste
- 500ml vegetable broth
- 400g can tomatoes, chopped
- 1 onion, chopped
- 2 garlic cloves, crushed or finely chopped
- 4 ancho chiles
- A pinch of saffron
- 1 lemon, juiced
- 300g paella rice
- 400g skinless, boneless chicken thighs, cut in half
- 300g chorizo, sliced
- 100g mussels, cleaned
- 100g frozen green pea

Instructions

1. Insert crisper plates in both drawers. Spray the crisper plates with nonstick cooking oil.
2. Toss the prawns and peppers with 1 tablespoon of olive oil, salt, and paprika.
3. Place the prawns in the zone 1 drawer and the peppers in the zone 2 drawer.
4. Select zone 1 and pair it with "AIR FRY" at 200°C for 6 minutes. Select zone 2 and pair it with "AIR FRY" at 190°C for 15 minutes. Select "SYNC" followed by the "START/STOP" button.
5. At the halfway point, gently stir the ingredients using a wooden spoon. Reinsert the drawers to resume cooking.
6. Meanwhile, bring the broth to a boil and cook paella rice according to the package instructions. Fluff your rice with a fork and transfer it to two baking tins that are previously greased with nonstick cooking oil.
7. Divide the other ingredients between baking tins. Cut roasted pepper into strips and add them to the baking tins, stir in the prawns and gently stir to combine.
8. Press the mussels in and add baking tins to the drawers.
9. Select zone 1 and pair it with "ROAST" at 180°C for 15 minutes. Select "MATCH" to duplicate settings across both zones. Press the "START/STOP" button.
10. At the halfway point, stir your paella with a wooden spoon and reinsert the drawers to resume cooking. Cook until the mussels have opened.
11. Check the seasoning, discard the mussels that stay shut, and serve warm. Enjoy!

Chicken Wings with Water Chestnuts

Prep time: 10 minutes
Cook time: 33 minutes
Serves 4

Per Serving:
Calories: 514
Fat: 26.5g
Carbs: 37.1g
Fibre: 0.5g
Protein: 30.3g

- 600g chicken wings, drumettes & flats
- 1 tbsp olive oil
- 1 tbsp corn flour
- 1 tsp garlic granules
- 1 tsp cayenne pepper
- Sea salt and ground black pepper, to taste
- 2 tbsp oyster sauce
- 2 tbsp honey
- 200g can water chestnuts, whole

Instructions
1. Insert crisper plates in both drawers. Spray the crisper plates with nonstick cooking oil.
2. Toss chicken wings with olive oil, corn flour, spices, oyster sauce and honey. Add the chicken to the zone 1 drawer and water chestnuts to the zone 2 drawer.
3. Select zone 1 and pair it with "AIR FRY" at 200°C for 33 minutes. Select zone 2 and pair it with "AIR FRY" at 190°C for 10 minutes. Select "SYNC" followed by the "START/STOP" button.
4. Cook until the tops of the wings are starting to char a little.

Bon appétit!

Queen's Coronation Chicken

Prep time: 10 minutes
Cook time: 12 minutes
Serves 4

Per Serving:
Calories: 555
Fat: 38.3g
Carbs: 16.8g
Fibre: 4.4g
Protein: 35.8g

- 600g chicken tenders
- 1 tbsp olive oil
- 1 tsp cayenne pepper
- 1 tsp mustard powder
- Sea salt and ground black pepper, to taste
- 1 tsp curry powder
- 100g mayonnaise
- 100g crème fraiche
- 2 tbsp mango chutney
- 1 tsp Worcestershire sauce
- 2 celery sticks, finely chopped
- 50g dried apricots, chopped
- 1 tbsp fresh parsley, chopped
- 1/2 tsp cumin
- 1 tsp fresh ginger, minced
- 60g almonds

Instructions
1. Toss the chicken with olive oil and spices in a grip seal bag; give them a good shake until everything is well covered.
2. Lower the chicken into the zone 1 drawer and the almonds into the zone 2 drawer,
3. Select zone 1 and pair it with "AIR FRY" at 200°C for 12 minutes. Select zone 2 and pair it with "ROAST" at 180°C for 5 minutes. Select "SYNC" followed by the "START/STOP" button.
4. At the half point, toss your ingredients to promote even cooking. Reinsert drawers to resume cooking.
5. Add the shredded chicken to a salad bowl; add the remaining ingredients and stir to coat in the sauce. Top with roasted almonds and serve. Bon appétit!

Somerset Cider Chicken

Prep time: 10 minutes
Cook time: 34 minutes
Serves 5

Per Serving:
Calories: 393
Fat: 12.8g
Carbs: 3.4g
Fibre: 0.4g
Protein: 61.6g

- 1.5kg whole chicken, skin-on, bone-in, cut into pieces
- 300ml cider
- Sea salt and ground black pepper, to taste
- 2 sprigs of thyme, plus more for garnish
- 1 tbsp English mustard powder
- 2 tbsp plain flour
- 2 tbsp butter, divided

Instructions
1. Mix the chicken with cider, salt, pepper, thyme, and mustard powder. Let the chicken marinade in your fridge for up to 12 hours.
2. Now, toss the chicken pieces with flour and 1 tablespoon of butter.
3. Select zone 1 and pair it with "ROAST" at 190°C for 34 minutes. Select "MATCH" to duplicate settings across both zones. Press the "START/STOP" button.
4. At the halfway point, turn the chicken over and baste it with the reserved marinade. Reinsert drawers to resume cooking.
5. Meanwhile, cook the reserved marinade with the remaining butter in a pan until the sauce has thickened. Serve warm chicken with the sauce on the side and enjoy!

Devilled Chicken

Prep time: 10 minutes
Cook time: 25 minutes
Serves 5

Per Serving:
Calories: 245
Fat: 6.5g
Carbs: 3.5g
Fibre: 0.7g
Protein: 41.3g

- 1kg chicken drumettes, bone-in, skin-on
- 2 garlic cloves
- 1 bay leaf
- Coarse sea salt and ground black pepper, to taste
- 1 tsp chilli powder
- 1/2 teaspoon turmeric powder
- 100ml tomato ketchup
- 1 tsp olive oil

Instructions
1. Pat the chicken drumettes dry using tea towels.
2. Crush the garlic and spices using a pestle and mortar. Rub the chicken with the oil, spice mix, and tomato ketchup.
3. Place the prepared chicken drumettes in the cooking basket, skin-side down.
4. Select zone 1 and pair it with "AIR FRY" at 190°C for 25 minutes. Select "MATCH" followed by the "START/STOP" button.
5. When zone 1 time reaches 15 minutes, turn them over, and baste with the remaining ketchup. Then, reinsert the drawers to continue cooking.

Bon appétit!

CHAPTER 3
MEAT

English Fry Up Skewers

Prep time: 10 minutes
Cook time: 15 minutes
Serves 4

Per Serving:
Calories: 493
Fat: 42.3g
Carbs: 8.5g
Fibre: 2.4g
Protein: 21.6g

- 400g button mushrooms, halved
- Sea salt and ground black pepper, to taste
- 4 pork sausages, smoked
- 20 cherry tomatoes
- 1 tsp paprika
- 4 rashers smoked bacon

Instructions
1. Toss the mushrooms and cherry tomatoes with salt, black pepper, and paprika. Insert a crisper plate in both drawers. Spray the plates with nonstick cooking oil.
2. Add the sausages and bacon to the zone 1 drawer; add the mushrooms and tomatoes to the zone 2 drawer.
3. Select zone 1 and pair it with "AIR FRY" at 200°C for 15 minutes. Select zone 2 and pair it with "AIR FRY" at 180°C for 10 minutes. Select "SYNC" followed by the "START/STOP" button.
4. Thread the ingredients onto the soaked wooden (or metal) skewers. Enjoy!

Hand-Raised Pork Pies

Prep time: 15 minutes
Cook time: 50 minutes
Serves 8

Per Serving:
Calories: 595
Fat: 36.3g
Carbs: 28.5g
Fibre: 1.2g
Protein: 35.6g

- Pastry:
- 100g lard
- 100ml water
- 1/2 tsp salt
- 300g plain flour
- 1 egg, beaten
- 3 gelatine leaves
- 200ml vegetable stock
- Filling:
- 800g pork mince, cooked
- 150g gammon, chopped
- 1 tbsp sage, chopped
- 1 large pinch of ground nutmeg
- Sea salt and ground black pepper, to taste

Instructions
1. In a small pan, bring the lard, water, and salt to a gentle boil. Stir the mixture into the flour using a wooden spoon.
2. When the batter is cool enough to handle, knead it well until smooth. Cut off 1/4 of the dough and wrap it in cling film.
3. Lightly flour the work surface and roll out the remaining dough to a circle (1/2cm thick). Fold the dough in thirds, roll and fold again.
4. Press the dough evenly into two springform cake tins. Mix the filling ingredients.
5. Fill the pies with the meat mixture; pack down well. Use the reserved dough to form the lids. Place on top of the pies and make a hole using a sharp knife.
6. Lower the tins into the cooking basket.
7. Select zone 1 and pair it with "BAKE" at 180°C for 30 minutes. Select "MATCH" followed by the "START/STOP" button.
8. Brush the top with beaten egg. Reduce the heat to 160°C fan and cook for 20 minutes more or until cooked through.
9. Soak the gelatine leaves in cold water for 5 to 10 minutes; squeeze out the excess water. Bring the vegetable stock to a gentle boil.
10. Heat off and immediately stir in the gelatine. Leave to cool to room temperature.
11. Pour the gelatine mixture into the pie through the hole in the top. Place your pies in the fridge to set overnight. Enjoy!

Simple Pork Chops

Prep time: 5 minutes
Cook time: 16 minutes
Serves 4

Per Serving:
Calories: 336
Fat: 9g
Carbs: 3.4g
Fibre: 0.5g
Protein: 55.3g

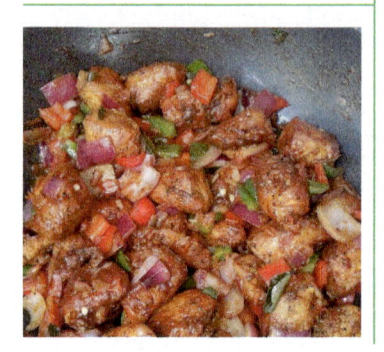

- 1 kg pork chops
- 2 tbsp Worcestershire sauce
- 1 tsp cayenne pepper
- Sea salt and ground black pepper, to taste
- 2 tbsp Sriracha
- 1 thumb-sized piece ginger, grated
- 2 garlic cloves, crushed

Instructions
1. Insert crisper plates in both drawers. Spray the crisper plates with nonstick cooking oil.
2. Toss pork chops with the other ingredients and lower them into the cooking basket.
3. Select zone 1 and pair it with "AIR FRY" at 200°C for 16 minutes. Select "MATCH" to duplicate settings across both zones. Press the "START/STOP" button.
4. At the halfway point, turn the pork chops over and reinsert the drawers to resume cooking.

Bon appétit

Pork Shoulder with Bubble and Squeak

Prep time: 10 minutes
Cook time: 1 hour 10 minutes
Serves 4

Per Serving:
Calories: 461
Fat: 25.6g
Carbs: 21.2g
Fibre: 3.8g
Protein: 34.9g

- 600g pork shoulder, cut into 2 pieces
- Sea salt and ground black pepper, to taste
- 300g potatoes, peeled and cut into wedges
- 1 tbsp lard
- 4 rashers back bacon, chopped
- 200g Brussels sprouts, chopped
- 1 thyme sprig, chopped
- 1 tbsp olive oil
- 1/2 tsp cayenne pepper
- 1 garlic clove, chopped
- 1 small leek, chopped
- Sea salt and ground black pepper, to taste

Instructions
1. Toss pork shoulder with olive oil and spices. Add the pork shoulder to the zone 1 drawer and potatoes to the zone 2 drawer.
2. Select zone 1 and pair it with "ROAST" at 175°C for 55 minutes. Select zone 2 and pair it with "ROAST" at 190°C for 20 minutes. Select "SYNC" followed by the "START/STOP" button.
3. At the halfway point, toss the ingredients and reinsert the drawers to resume cooking.
4. Mash the potatoes and combine them with the other ingredients. Divide the mixture between two baking tins and lower them into the cooking basket.
5. Bake your Bubble and Squeak for about 15 minutes or until cooked through.
6. Shred the pork with two forks. Pile into plates along with Bubble and Squeak. Bon appétit!

Classic Steak Pie

Prep time: 10 minutes
Cook time: 45 minutes
Serves 6

Per Serving:
Calories: 594
Fat: 32.6g
Carbs: 40.4g
Fibre: 4.3g
Protein: 38.3g

- 600g braising steak, diced
- 2 tbsp plain flour
- Sea salt and ground black pepper, to taste
- 1 tsp paprika
- 2 shallots, sliced
- 200g gammon, chopped
- 2 (350g) jars red wine sauce
- 200ml hot vegetable (or chicken) stock
- 1 pack (320g) frozen puff pastry, defrosted
- 1 egg, beaten

Instructions
1. Pat the meat dry with tea towels.
2. In two baking trays (or casserole dishes), toss the steak with the flour and a generous amount of salt, black pepper, and paprika.
3. Next, add the shallots, gammon, wine sauce, and stock.
4. Select zone 1 and pair it with "AIR FRY" at 200°C for 20 minutes. Select "MATCH" to duplicate settings across both zones. Press the "START/STOP" button.
5. Then, roll out two pieces of your pastry to a slightly larger size than the baking trays. Lay the pastry over the top, sealing well.
6. Create a steam hole in the centre, brush the top with egg wash and continue to bake for a further 25 minutes at 180°C. Enjoy!

Beef Wellington Wontons

Prep time: 10 minutes
Cook time: 35 minutes
Serves 6

Per Serving:
Calories: 574
Fat: 22.6g
Carbs: 54.4g
Fibre: 2.6g
Protein: 37.3g

- 20g butter
- 200g brown mushrooms, chopped
- 1 medium leek, finely chopped
- 800g beef mince
- 100g tomato paste
- 2 garlic cloves, finely chopped
- 2 large eggs
- Sea salt and ground black pepper, to taste
- 1 tbsp coriander, chopped
- 16 wonton wrappers, 9cm square, thawed if frozen

Instructions
1. Thoroughly combine the butter, mushrooms, leek, beef, tomato paste, garlic, one egg, salt, black pepper, and coriander.
2. Press the mixture into two lightly-greased baking trays.
3. Select zone 1 and pair it with "ROAST" at 200°C for 20 minutes. Select "MATCH" to duplicate settings across both zones. Press the "START/STOP" button.
4. Meanwhile, beat the remaining egg with a little water.
5. Divide the ingredients between wonton wrappers; brush with the egg wash and place them on the baking tray.
6. Select zone 1 and pair it with "ROAST" at 175°C for 15 minutes. Select "MATCH" to duplicate settings across both zones. Press the "START/STOP" button.

Bon appétit!

British Beef Jerky

Prep time: 10 minutes
Cook time: 7 hours
Serves 8

Per Serving:
Calories: 65
Fat: 1.3g
Carbs: 2.5g
Fibre: 0.4g
Protein: 10.3g

- 400g sirloin steak, thinly sliced
- 10ml Worcestershire sauce
- 1 tbsp liquid smoke
- 1 tbsp honey
- 1 tsp garlic granules
- 1 tsp onion powder
- 1 tsp chilli flakes

Instructions
1. Add all the ingredients to a large ceramic (or glass bowl). Cover the bowl and place in your fridge overnight.
2. Place a single layer of the beef slices in the cooking basket. Then add the crisper plate to the drawer on top of the ingredients; arrange another layer of beef slices on the crisper plate.
3. Select zone 1 and pair it with "DEHYDRATE" at 70°C for 7 hours. Select "MATCH" followed by the "START/STOP" button.

Chorizo-Stuffed Pork Loin

Prep time: 10 minutes
Cook time: 55 minutes
Serves 4

Per Serving:
Calories: 477
Fat: 24.9g
Carbs: 5.1g
Fibre: 0.9g
Protein: 55.4g

- 800g pork loin, boned, cut into four pieces
- 1 tsp olive oil
- 1 tsp cayenne pepper
- Sea salt and ground black pepper, to taste
- 1 lemon, freshly squeezed
- 1 small pack sage, leaves roughly chopped
- 1 small pack parsley, leaves roughly chopped
- 5 garlic cloves, peeled and cut into thin slivers
- 160g chorizo, crumbled

Instructions
1. Toss pork loin with olive oil and spices.
2. Score the skin of the pork loin in a crisscross pattern using a sharp knife. Cut a slit along the side of the loin to open it out. Brush it with the lemon juice.
3. Add the sage, parsley, garlic, and chorizo. Roll them up and secure them tightly with string in 3-4cm intervals.
4. Select zone 1 and pair it with "AIR FRY" at 195°C for 55 minutes. Select "MATCH" to duplicate settings across both zones. Press the "START/STOP" button.

Bon appétit!

Roast Pork Roulade

Prep time: 10 minutes
Cook time: 50 minutes
Serves 5

Per Serving:
Calories: 427
Fat: 29g
Carbs: 1.4g
Fibre: 0.3g
Protein: 39.4g

- 800g pork loin cut into two pieces
- 1 tsp olive oil
- 1 tsp dried rosemary
- 1 tsp paprika
- Sea salt and ground black pepper, to taste
- 50g fresh breadcrumbs
- 200g good quality sausages, skinned
- 50 ml veal stock

Instructions
1. Brush the pork loin with olive oil and add spices. Using a sharp knife, cut down the length of the meat, then open both pieces out like a book.
2. Add the remaining ingredients, except the vial stock. Roll them up and secure them tightly.
3. Select zone 1 and pair it with "AIR FRY" at 195°C for 50 minutes. Select "MATCH" to duplicate settings across both zones. Press the "START/STOP" button.
4. At the half point, baste the pork with the veal stock. Reinsert drawers to resume cooking.
5. Leave the pork to rest for about 30 minutes before carving.

Bon appétit!

Homemade Pork Burgers with Chips

Prep time: 10 minutes
Cook time: 22 minutes
Serves 3

Per Serving:
Calories: 669
Fat: 33.4g
Carbs: 60g
Fibre: 6.5g
Protein: 31.9g

- 400g pork mince
- 1 large onion, chopped
- 2 garlic cloves, minced
- 100g fresh breadcrumbs
- Sea salt and ground black pepper, to taste
- 1 tsp cayenne pepper
- 1 tsp mustard powder
- 500g potatoes, cut into chips
- 2 tsp olive oil

Instructions
1. Insert a crisper plate in each drawer. Spray the crisper plates with nonstick cooking oil.
2. Thoroughly combine the pork mince, onion, garlic, breadcrumbs, and spices. Shape the mixture into three patties.
3. Add burgers to the zone 1 drawer and potatoes to the zone 2 drawer. Now, brush them with olive oil.
4. Select zone 1 and pair it with "AIR FRY" at 190°C for 22 minutes. Select "MATCH" to duplicate settings across both zones. Press the "START/STOP" button.
5. When zone 1 time reaches 11 minutes, turn the ingredients over and reinsert the drawers to continue cooking.
6. Serve your burgers in the buns garnished with warm chips.

Bon appétit!

Pork Cutlets with Broccoli

Prep time: 5 minutes
Cook time: 16 minutes
Serves 4

Per Serving:
Calories: 339
Fat: 11.9g
Carbs: 10.4g
Fibre: 3.2g
Protein: 47.7g

- 800g pork cutlets
- 1 tsp English mustard
- 2 tbsp soy sauce
- 1 tsp paprika
- Sea salt and ground black pepper, to taste
- 400g broccoli florets
- 1 tsp garlic granules
- 2 tsp olive oil

Instructions
1. Insert crisper plates in both drawers. Spray the crisper plates with nonstick cooking oil.
2. Toss pork cutlets with mustard, soy sauce, paprika, salt, and pepper; brush them with 1 teaspoon of olive oil and lower them into the zone 1 drawer.
3. Toss broccoli florets with the remaining 1 teaspoon of olive oil and arrange them in the zone 2 drawer.
4. Select zone 1 and pair it with "AIR FRY" at 200°C for 16 minutes. Select zone 2 and pair it with "ROAST" at 190°C for 8 minutes. Select "SYNC" followed by the "START/STOP" button.
5. At the half point, toss your ingredients to promote even cooking. Reinsert drawers to resume cooking.

Bon appétit

Roast Beef with Pickled Red Cabbage

Prep time: 30 minutes
Cook time: 55 minutes
Serves 4

Per Serving:
Calories: 348
Fat: 11.7g
Carbs: 27.1g
Fibre: 4.6g
Protein: 34.4g

- 600g beef rump roast, cut into 2 pieces
- 400g new potatoes
- 2 tsp olive oil
- 1 tsp garlic granules
- 1 tsp dried rosemary
- 1 tsp paprika
- Sea salt and ground black pepper, to taste
- 200g pickled red cabbage
- 1 jalapeño, thinly sliced
- 1 small Granny Smith apple, sliced
- 2 tbsp fresh parsley, chopped

Instructions
1. Toss the beef and potatoes with olive oil and spices. Place the beef in the zone 1 drawer and the potatoes in the zone 2 drawer.
2. Select zone 1 and pair it with "ROAST" at 195°C for 55 minutes. Select zone 2 and pair it with "ROAST" at 190°C for 20 minutes. Select "SYNC" followed by the "START/STOP" button.
3. At the half point, turn your ingredients over to promote even cooking. Reinsert drawers to resume cooking.
4. Meanwhile, combine the cabbage with jalapeño, apple, and parsley.
5. Leave the beef to rest for about 30 minutes before carving.

Bon appétit!

Steak Tips with Dried Tomato Pesto

Prep time: 2 hour
Cook time: 25 minutes
Serves 4

Per Serving:
Calories: 580
Fat: 37.2g
Carbs: 20.7g
Fibre: 4.8g
Protein: 41.5g

- 600g steak tips
- 1 tbsp olive oil
- 100ml dry red wine
- 2 tbsp soy sauce
- 2 garlic cloves, crushed
- 1 tsp chipotle chilli paste
- Sea salt and ground black pepper, to taste
- 300g tomatoes
- Dried Tomato Pesto:
- 4 sun-dried tomatoes
- 50g almonds
- 100g sun-dried tomatoes
- 2 cloves garlic, sliced
- 50g grated Parmesan cheese
- 50ml extra-virgin olive oil
- Kosher salt and ground black pepper, to taste

Instructions
1. In a ceramic bowl, place the steak tips, olive oil, wine, soy sauce, garlic, chilli paste, salt, and black pepper. Leave to marinate for at least 2 hours.
2. Place the steak tips in the zone 1 drawer and reserve the marinade.
3. Brush your tomatoes with cooking oil; place them in the zone 2 drawer.
4. Select zone 1 and pair it with "AIR FRY" at 200°C for 25 minutes. Select zone 2 and pair it with "ROAST" at 200°C for 8 minutes. Select "SYNC" followed by the "START/STOP" button.
5. At the halfway point, turn the steaks over and baste them with the reserved marinade; reinsert the drawers to resume cooking.
6. Then, make the pesto by mixing the roasted tomatoes and ingredients in your blender or food processor. Place the pesto in your fridge until ready to serve.
7. Serve warm steak tips with chilled pesto and enjoy!

Spiced Pork Medallions

Prep time: 5 minutes
Cook time: 16 minutes
Serves 4

Per Serving:
Calories: 336
Fat: 9g
Carbs: 3.4g
Fibre: 0.5g
Protein: 55.3g

- 1 kg pork medallions
- 1 tsp paprika
- Sea salt and ground black pepper, to taste
- 2 tbsp sweet chilli sauce
- 1 thumb-sized piece ginger, grated
- 2 garlic cloves, crushed

Instructions
1. Insert crisper plates in both drawers. Spray the crisper plates with nonstick cooking oil.
2. Toss pork medallions with the other ingredients and lower them into the cooking basket.
3. Select zone 1 and pair it with "AIR FRY" at 200°C for 16 minutes. Select "MATCH" to duplicate settings across both zones. Press the "START/STOP" button.
4. At the halfway point, turn the pork medallions over and reinsert the drawers to resume cooking.

Bon appétit

CHAPTER 4
FISH & SEAFOOD

Blackened Shrimp

Prep time: 10 minutes
Cook time: 12 minutes
Serves 4

Per Serving:
Calories: 196
Fat: 4.9g
Carbs: 8.6g
Fibre: 3.7g
Protein: 33.9g

- 600g shrimp
- 2 garlic cloves, crushed
- 1 tsp paprika
- 1 thyme sprig, chopped
- 1 rosemary sprig, leaves picked and chopped
- Sea salt and ground black pepper, to taste
- 1 medium lime, freshly squeezed
- 2 tbsp extra-virgin olive oil
- 600g asparagus, deseeded and halved

Instructions
1. Insert crisper plates in both drawers and spray them with cooking oil.
2. Toss the shrimp and asparagus with the remaining ingredients.
3. Add the shrimp to the zone 1 drawer and the asparagus to the zone 2 drawer.
4. Select zone 1 and pair it with "AIR FRY" at 200°C for 12 minutes. Select zone 2 and pair it with "AIR FRY" at 200°C for 5 minutes. Select "SYNC" followed by the "START/STOP" button.
5. Shake the drawers halfway through the cooking time to ensure even cooking. Enjoy!

Salmon, Potato & Leek Traybake

Prep time: 10 minutes
Cook time: 20 minutes
Serves 4

Per Serving:
Calories: 400
Fat: 10.2g
Carbs: 40.5g
Fibre: 5.2g
Protein: 35.3g

- 600g salmon fillets
- 1 medium leek, sliced
- 4 medium potatoes, peeled and cut into 1.5cm pieces
- 1 medium celery stalk, trimmed and cut into 1.5cm pieces
- 1 tbsp olive oil
- 1/2 tsp hot paprika
- 1 tsp garlic granules
- 1 tsp onion powder
- Sea salt and ground black pepper, to taste

Instructions
1. Toss the salmon and vegetables with olive oil and spices until they are well coated on all sides.
2. Place the salmon in the zone 1 drawer (with a lightly greased crisper plate).
3. Arrange the vegetable in a lightly greased roasting tin; add the roasting tin to the zone 2 drawer (with no crisper plate inserted).
4. Select zone 1 and pair it with "AIR FRY" at 190°C for 12 minutes. Select zone 2 and pair it with "ROAST" at 190°C for 20 minutes. Select "SYNC" followed by the "START/STOP" button.
5. When zone 1 time reaches 8 minutes, turn the salmon fillets over and spray them with nonstick cooking oil on the other side; reinsert the drawer to continue cooking.
6. When zone 2 time reaches 10 minutes, remove the leek and reinsert the drawer to continue cooking.
7. Top your vegetables with salmon and serve from the tin in the middle of the table. Bon appétit!

Cod Fillets with Horseradish Sauce

Prep time: 10 minutes
Cook time: 20 minutes
Serves 4

Per Serving:
Calories: 573
Fat: 28g
Carbs: 52.5g
Fibre: 7.3g
Protein: 27.5g

- 4 (220g each) codfish fillets
- 120g fresh breadcrumbs
- 1 tbsp rosemary, chopped
- 1 tbsp olive oil
- Horseradish Sauce:
- 2 tbsp hot horseradish
- 1 tbsp cider vinegar
- 1 large egg, beaten
- 1 tbsp fresh cilantro, chopped
- Sea salt and ground black pepper, to taste
- 150g plain flour
- 150ml crème fraîche
- 1 tbsp dill, chopped

Instructions
1. Pat the codfish fillets dry with tea towels.
2. Create the breading station: Beat the egg until pale and frothy. In a separate shallow dish, place the flour. Mix the breadcrumbs with the herbs, salt, and pepper in a third dish.
3. Coat the fish fillets in the flour. Dip fish fillets in the beaten eggs; roll them over the breadcrumb mixture.
4. Arrange the prepared fish fillets on the lightly greased crisper plates. Brush them with olive oil.
5. Select zone 1 and pair it with "AIR FRY" at 185°C for 20 minutes. Select "MATCH" to duplicate settings across both zones. Press the "START/STOP" button.
6. When zone 1 time reaches 9 minutes, turn the fish fillets over to promote even cooking. Reinsert the drawers to continue cooking and cook until the topping is crispy.
7. In the meantime, make the Horseradish Sauce by mixing the ingredients.
8. Serve warm cod fillets on a serving tray with the Horseradish Sauce on the side.

Bon appétit!

Parmesan Crusted Tuna

Prep time: 10 minutes
Cook time: 17 minutes
Serves 4

Per Serving:
Calories: 532
Fat: 24.7g
Carbs: 7g
Fibre: 0.3g
Protein: 67.2g

- 1 kg tuna steaks
- 1 tsp sweet paprika
- 1 tsp dried parsley flakes
- 1 tsp garlic granules
- Sea salt and ground black pepper, to taste
- 1 tsp olive oil
- 1 tbsp fresh lime juice
- 150g parmesan cheese, preferably freshly grated

Instructions
1. Insert crisper plates in both drawers. Spray crisper plates with nonstick cooking oil.
2. Toss tuna steaks with spices, olive oil, and lemon juice. Place tuna steaks in the cooking basket.
3. Select zone 1 and pair it with "AIR FRY" at 190°C for 17 minutes. Select "MATCH" to duplicate settings across both zones. Press the "START/STOP" button.
4. When zone 1 time reaches 9 minutes, turn the steaks over and sprinkle them with the grated parmesan. Reinsert the drawers to continue cooking.
5. Taste and adjust the seasonings.

Bon appétit!

Salmon with Capers

Prep time: 10 minutes
Cook time: 12 minutes
Serves 4

Per Serving:
Calories: 257
Fat: 8.7g
Carbs: 1.7g
Fibre: 0.3g
Protein: 40.6g

- 800g salmon fillets
- 1 tsp garlic granules
- Sea salt and ground black pepper, to taste
- 1 tsp olive oil
- 1 tbsp fresh lime juice
- 1 small jar of capers in brine

Instructions
1. Insert crisper plates in both drawers. Spray crisper plates with nonstick cooking oil.
2. Toss salmon with spices, olive oil, and lime juice. Place them in the cooking basket.
3. Select zone 1 and pair it with "AIR FRY" at 190°C for 12 minutes. Select "MATCH" to duplicate settings across both zones. Press the "START/STOP" button.
4. When zone 1 time reaches 6 minutes, turn the salmon fillets over and sprinkle them with capers. Reinsert the drawers to continue cooking.
5. Taste and adjust the seasonings.

Bon appétit!

Crab Cakes with Garlic Mayo

Prep time: 10 minutes
Cook time: 12 minutes
Serves 4

Per Serving:
Calories: 450
Fat: 10.1g
Carbs: 56.5g
Fibre: 3.5g
Protein: 30.5g

- 400g crab meat, chopped
- 1 large slice of white bread, soaked in 2 tbsp of milk
- 2 large eggs, beaten
- 1 large shallot, chopped
- 2 garlic cloves, pressed (or chopped green garlic)
- 2 tbsp fresh coriander, finely chopped
- Sea salt and ground black pepper, to taste
- 1 tsp mustard powder
- 100g plain flour
- 150g dried breadcrumbs
- Garlic Mayo:
- 100ml mayonnaise
- 1 tsp dried dill
- 4 garlic cloves, crushed

Instructions
1. Insert crisper plates in both drawers. Line the crisper plates with baking parchment.
2. In a mixing bowl, thoroughly combine the crab meat, bread, eggs, shallot, garlic, coriander, salt, black pepper, and mustard powder.
3. Afterwards, add the flour and mix to combine well. Roll the fish mixture into small patties.
4. Add dried breadcrumbs to a shallow dish; then, roll the patties over the breadcrumbs and lower them onto the prepared crisper plates.
5. Select zone 1 and pair it with "AIR FRY" at 200°C for 12 minutes. Select "MATCH" to duplicate settings across both zones. Press the "START/STOP" button.
6. When zone 1 time reaches 6 minutes, turn the patties over to promote even cooking. Reinsert the drawers to continue cooking.
7. Meanwhile, make the garlic mayo by mixing the ingredients. Spoon the chilled mayo over each crab cake and enjoy!

Crab-Stuffed Avocado

Prep time: 10 minutes
Cook time: 11 minutes
Serves 6

Per Serving:
Calories: 335
Fat: 25.8g
Carbs: 9.7g
Fibre: 6.9g
Protein: 18.9g

- 3 large avocados, pitted and cut in half
- 3 medium eggs
- 200g crab meat
- Sea salt and ground black pepper, to taste
- 1 tsp mustard powder
- 1/2 tsp garlic granules
- 160g gruyere cheese, crumbled

Instructions
1. Cut the avocados in half and carefully remove the pits. Scoop out about 2 tablespoons of avocado flesh from the centre of each half and set it aside.
2. Whisk the eggs with the reserved avocado flesh, crab meat, and spices. Spoon the mixture into each avocado cup.
3. Lower them into the cooking basket.
4. Select zone 1 and pair it with "BAKE" at 200°C for 11 minutes. Select "MATCH" followed by the "START/STOP" button.
5. At the halfway point, top avocado halves with cheese. Reinsert drawers to resume cooking. Enjoy!

Glazed Garlic Prawns

Prep time: 10 minutes
Cook time: 10 minutes
Serves 4

Per Serving:
Calories: 225
Fat: 3.5g
Carbs: 7.7g
Fibre: 0.8g
Protein: 40.9g

- 800g tiger prawns, peeled, tails on
- 2 garlic cloves, crushed
- 1 medium lemon, juiced
- 2 tbsp dry sherry wine
- 1 tbsp honey
- 1 tbsp paprika
- Sea salt and ground black pepper, to your liking
- 2 tsp sesame oil

Instructions
1. Toss tiger prawns with the other ingredients.
2. Place the prawns in the cooking basket (with a crisper plate inserted).
3. Select zone 1 and pair it with "AIR FRY" at 200°C for 10 minutes. Select "MATCH" followed by the "START/STOP" button.
4. When zone 1 time reaches 5 minutes, turn the prawns over using silicone-tipped tongs.
5. Serve immediately and enjoy!

British Scampi

Prep time: 10 minutes
Cook time: 12 minutes
Serves 4

Per Serving:
Calories: 145
Fat: 4.7g
Carbs: 20.7g
Fibre: 2.2g
Protein: 5.5g

- 16 langoustine (or Dublin Bay prawn tails)
- Sea salt and ground black pepper, to taste
- 1 tsp paprika
- 100g cornflour
- 1 tbsp olive oil

Instructions
1. Insert crisper plates in both drawers. Spray the crisper plates with nonstick cooking oil.
2. Mix the cornflour with spices in a shallow dish.
3. Pat the scampi dry with tea (paper) towels; toss them in the cornflour mixture.
4. Place your scampi in both drawers. Spray them with nonstick cooking oil.
5. Select zone 1 and pair it with "AIR FRY" at 180°C for 12 minutes. Select "MATCH" to duplicate settings across both zones. Press the "START/STOP" button.
6. When zone 1 time reaches 6 minutes, shake the drawer for approximately 10 seconds to ensure even cooking. Reinsert the drawer to continue cooking.

Bon appétit!

Garlic Lemon King Scallops

Prep time: 10 minutes
Cook time: 12 minutes
Serves 4

Per Serving:
Calories: 225
Fat: 7.9g
Carbs: 16.6g
Fibre: 1.9g
Protein: 19.4g

- 600g king scallops
- 2 large garlic cloves, peeled
- 1 rosemary sprig, leaves picked
- Sea salt and ground black pepper, to taste
- 1 medium lemon, freshly squeezed
- 2 tbsp extra-virgin olive oil
- 400g onions, quartered

Instructions
1. Insert crisper plates in both drawers and spray them with cooking oil.
2. Toss the scallops and onion with the remaining ingredients.
3. Add the scallops to the zone 1 drawer and the onions to the zone 2 drawer.
4. Select zone 1 and pair it with "AIR FRY" at 200°C for 12 minutes. Select zone 2 and pair it with "AIR FRY" at 190°C for 10 minutes. Select "SYNC" followed by the "START/STOP" button.
5. Shake the drawers halfway through the cooking time to ensure even cooking. Enjoy!

Fish Cakes with Asparagus

Prep time: 10 minutes
Cook time: 15 minutes
Serves 4

Per Serving:
Calories: 406
Fat: 10.4g
Carbs: 54.6g
Fibre: 5.6g
Protein: 23.4g

- 300g Maris Piper potatoes, peeled and grated
- 300g skinned haddock fillets, flaked
- 1 tbsp fresh parsley leaves, chopped
- 100g plain flour
- 400g asparagus, trimmed
- 60ml milk
- 1 large egg, beaten
- 100g breadcrumbs
- 2 tbsp olive oil

Instructions
1. Place the potatoes in a medium saucepan and cover them with hot water. Bring it to a boil and immediately turn the heat to a medium-low. Let your potatoes simmer for about 12 minutes, until fork-tender.
2. Insert a crisper plate in each drawer. Spray the crisper plates with nonstick cooking oil.
3. Mash your potatoes with a fork and then, add the flaked fish, milk, parsley, egg, and flour.
4. Place the breadcrumbs in a shallow dish. Shape the mixture into small patties; roll them over the breadcrumbs and brush them with 1 tablespoon of olive oil.
5. Brush your asparagus with the remaining 1 tablespoon of olive oil
6. Add the fish cakes to the zone 1 drawer and asparagus to the zone 2 drawer.
7. Select zone 1 and pair it with "AIR FRY" at 200°C for 15 minutes. Select zone 2 and pair it with "AIR FRY" at 200°C for 5 minutes. Select "SYNC" followed by the "START/STOP" button.

Bon appétit!

Fish Tacos

Prep time: 10 minutes
Cook time: 20 minutes
Serves 4

Per Serving:
Calories: 434
Fat: 10g
Carbs: 53.4g
Fibre: 4.4g
Protein: 33.6g

- 500g tilapia fillets
- 4 bell peppers, deseeded and halved
- 1 tbsp olive oil
- 1 tsp taco spice mix
- Sea salt and ground black pepper, to taste
- 1 small onion, sliced
- 100ml salsa
- 4 medium tortillas

Instructions
1. Toss tilapia fillets and bell peppers with olive oil and spices. Add the fish to the zone 1 drawer and bell peppers to the zone 2 drawer.
2. Select zone 1 and pair it with "AIR FRYER" at 200°C for 12 minutes. Select zone 2 and pair it with "ROAST" at 180°C for 15 minutes. Select "SYNC" followed by the "START/STOP" button.
3. At the halfway point, turn the fish and peppers over and reinsert the drawers to resume cooking; cut the fish and peppers into strips.
4. Pile air-fried fish and pepper into tortillas along with onions and salsa.
5. Add tortillas to both drawers. Select "REHEAT" at 170°C for 5 minutes. Serve immediately and enjoy!

Halibut and Chickpea Salad

Prep time: 10 minutes
Cook time: 15 minutes
Serves 5

Per Serving:
Calories: 481
Fat: 22.2g
Carbs: 41.2g
Fibre: 8.1g
Protein: 30.2g

- 600g halibut steaks
- 1 tsp hot paprika
- 1 tsp dried onion flakes
- 1 tsp garlic granules
- Sea salt and ground black pepper, to taste
- 300g chickpeas, drained
- 2 tsp olive oil
- 1 tbsp fresh lime juice
- 1 large tomato, diced
- 1 medium onion, sliced
- 1 small cucumber, sliced

Instructions
1. Insert crisper plates in both drawers. Spray crisper plates with nonstick cooking oil.
2. Toss halibut steaks with spices, 1 teaspoon of olive oil, and lime juice. Toss canned chickpeas with the remaining 1 teaspoon of olive oil, salt, and black pepper.
3. Place halibut steaks in the zone 1 drawer and the chickpeas in the zone 2 drawer.
4. Select zone 1 and pair it with "AIR FRY" at 200°C for 12 minutes. Select zone 2 and pair it with "ROAST" at 200°C for 15 minutes. Select "SYNC" followed by the "START/STOP" button.
5. At the halfway point, toss your food to promote even cooking; reinsert the drawers to resume cooking.
6. To make your salad, add the fish strips and chickpeas to a salad bowl; add the other ingredients and toss to combine.
7. Serve immediately and enjoy!

Fish & Chips Burger

Prep time: 10 minutes
Cook time: 25 minutes
Serves 3

Per Serving:
Calories: 644
Fat: 10.3g
Carbs: 96.1g
Fibre: 8.3g
Protein: 40.2g

- 3 (180g each) sea bass fillets, skinless and boneless
- 1 tsp hot paprika
- 1 tsp onion flakes
- 1/2 tsp garlic granules
- Sea salt and ground black pepper, to taste
- 60g plain flour
- 1 large egg, beaten
- 60g fresh breadcrumbs
- 2 tsp olive oil
- 3 soft rolls
- 1 medium sweet potato, peeled and cut into sticks

Instructions
1. Pat fish fillets dry using paper towels; then, coat the fish fillets in spices with your hands.
2. Now, create the breading station: Add the flour to a shallow bowl. Whisk the egg until it is well beaten. In a third shallow bowl, place the breadcrumbs.
3. Dust fish fillets with the flour. Dip fish fillets in the egg, and then, roll them over the breadcrumbs.
4. Arrange the fish fillets in zone 1 drawer and the potatoes in zone 2 drawer; brush them with olive oil.
5. Select zone 1 and pair it with "AIR FRY" at 200°C for 15 minutes. Select zone 2 and pair it with "AIR FRY" at 190°C for 25 minutes. Select "SYNC" followed by the "START/STOP" button.
6. At the halfway point, toss the ingredients to ensure even cooking. Reinsert drawers to resume cooking.
7. Top soft rolls with fish fillets and potatoes. You can add toppings of choice. Bon appétit!

CHAPTER 5
BEANS & GRAINS

Spicy Garlic Croutons

Prep time: 10 minutes
Cook time: 6 minutes
Serves 3

Per Serving:
Calories: 126
Fat: 5.5g
Carbs: 16.1g
Fibre: 1.8g
Protein: 2.8g

- 3 thick slices of sourdough or bloomer, cut into 2cm cubes
- 1 tbsp olive oil
- 2 garlic cloves, crushed
- A pinch of dried oregano
- Sea salt to taste

Instructions
1. Toss bread cubes with the other ingredients. Arrange them in the cooking basket.
2. Select zone 1 and pair it with "BAKE" at 200°C for 6 minutes. Select "MATCH" to duplicate settings across both zones. Press the "START/STOP" button.
3. When zone 1 time reaches 3 minutes, shake the drawer for approximately 10 seconds to ensure even cooking. Reinsert the drawer to continue cooking.

Bon appétit!

Paprika Roasted Chickpeas

Prep time: 10 minutes
Cook time: 15 minutes
Serves 8

Per Serving:
Calories: 90
Fat: 2.6g
Carbs: 8g
Fibre: 2.4g
Protein: 2.5g

- 1 (400g) can chickpeas, drained and rinsed
- 1 tbsp paprika
- 1 tbsp olive oil
- 1 tsp garlic granules
- Sea salt and ground black pepper, to taste

Instructions
1. Toss the chickpeas with the remaining ingredients.
2. Place the chickpeas in the cooking basket.
3. Select zone 1 and pair it with "ROAST" at 200°C for 15 minutes. Select "MATCH" to duplicate settings across both zones. Press the "START/STOP" button.
4. When zone 1 time reaches 8 minutes, shake the drawers to ensure even browning; reinsert the drawers to continue cooking.
5. Serve roasted chickpeas and enjoy!

Beans on Toast

Prep time: 5 minutes
Cook time: 8 minutes
Serves 5

Per Serving:
Calories: 477
Fat: 21.1g
Carbs: 60g
Fibre: 11.8g
Protein: 1.1g

- 1 loaf of crusty bread, sliced
- 20ml extra-virgin olive oil
- Sea salt and ground black pepper, to taste
- 1 tsp paprika
- 1 tsp garlic granules
- 200g canned pinto beans

Instructions
1. Toss the bread slices with olive oil, salt, black pepper, paprika, and garlic granules.
2. Place the bread slices in the cooking basket.
3. Select zone 1 and pair it with "AIR FRY" at 180°C for 5 minutes. Select "MATCH" to duplicate settings across both zones. Press the "START/STOP" button.
4. Top warm toasted bread with beans. Add them to the cooking basket. Select "REHEAT" at 170°C for 3 minutes.
5. Serve immediately and enjoy!

Lentil and Coriander Burger with Chips

Prep time: 10 minutes
Cook time: 40 minutes
Serves 6

Per Serving:
Calories: 420
Fat: 5.1g
Carbs: 77.5g
Fibre: 12.2g
Protein: 17.1g

- 1 (400g) can red lentils, rinsed and drained
- 300g quinoa, soaked overnight and rinsed
- 1 medium onion, peeled
- 2 garlic cloves
- 100g tortilla chips, crushed
- 1 tsp smoked paprika
- 1 tsp coriander seeds, ground
- Sea salt and ground black pepper, to taste
- Chips:
- 2 medium potatoes, peeled and cut into sticks
- 1 tsp olive oil

Instructions
1. Insert the crisper plates in both drawers and spray them with cooking oil.
2. In your blender, process all the ingredients until a thick and uniform batter is formed. Shape the mixture into equal patties.
3. Now, spray the patties with nonstick cooking oil and then, place them on the crisper plates.
4. Select zone 1 and pair it with "AIR FRY" at 190°C for 20 minutes. Select "MATCH" to duplicate settings across both zones. Press the "START/STOP" button.
5. When zone 1 time reaches 10 minutes, turn the patties over and spray them with cooking oil on the other side; then, reinsert the drawers to continue cooking.
6. Toss potatoes with 1 teaspoon of olive oil and salt. Select zone 1 and pair it with "AIR FRY" at 190°C for 20 minutes. Select "MATCH" to duplicate settings across both zones. Press the "START/STOP" button.
7. Serve warm patties with chips and enjoy!

British Baked Beans

Prep time: 10 minutes
Cook time: 20 minutes
Serves 6

Per Serving:
Calories: 537
Fat: 33.5g
Carbs: 34.5g
Fibre: 9.2g
Protein: 25.7g

- 1 tsp olive oil
- 2 (400g) cans cannellini beans, drained
- 1 red bell pepper, seeded and chopped
- 1 large onion, chopped
- 2 garlic cloves, minced
- 1 bay leaf
- 450g pureed tomatoes
- 2 tsp bouillon powder
- 1/4 tsp coriander seeds, ground
- 600g Italian sausages

Instructions
1. Brush the inside of an oven-safe baking tin with olive oil. Add the beans, pepper, onions, garlic, bay leaf, pureed tomatoes, bouillon powder, and coriander seeds.
2. Place the baking tin in the zone 1 drawer. Place the sausages in the zone 2 drawer.
3. Select zone 1 and pair it with "BAKE" at 180°C for 20 minutes. Select zone 2 and pair it with "AIRFRY" at 200°C for 16 minutes. Select "SYNC" followed by the "START/STOP" button.
4. When zone 1 time reaches 10 minutes, stir the beans, and reinsert the drawers to continue cooking.
5. When zone 2 time reaches 8 minutes, flip the sausages over to ensure even browning; reinsert drawers to continue cooking.

Bon appétit!

Griddle Scones with Clotted Cream

Prep time: 10 minutes
Cook time: 20 minutes
Serves 6

Per Serving:
Calories: 220
Fat: 8.5g
Carbs: 31.3g
Fibre: 2.5g
Protein: 4.4g

- 500g new potatoes, scrubbed
- 25g butter, softened
- 1/2 tsp cayenne pepper
- Sea salt and ground black pepper, to taste
- 120g plain flour (plus more for rolling)
- 1 tsp baking powder
- 100ml clotted cream, to serve

Instructions
1. Add new potatoes to the cooking basket.
2. Select zone 1 and pair it with "AIR FRY" at 190°C for 20 minutes. Select "MATCH" to duplicate settings across both zones. Press the "START/STOP" button.
3. When zone 1 time reaches 10 minutes, turn the patties over and spray them with cooking oil on the other side; then, reinsert the drawers to continue cooking.
4. Mash the potatoes and add the other ingredients. Mix until a dough ball forms.
5. Turn the prepared dough out onto a lightly floured surface and separate it into 2 balls.
6. Pat each ball out into a flat circle, turning and lightly flouring each side so that it doesn't stick. Prick both circles all over with a fork and place them on a parchment-lined cooking basket.
7. Select zone 1 and pair it with "BAKE" at 190°C for 20 minutes. Select "MATCH" to duplicate settings across both zones. Press the "START/STOP" button.
8. Serve with clotted cream and enjoy!

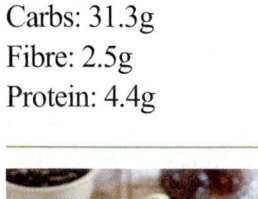

Staffordshire Oat Cake

Prep time: 10 minutes
Cook time: 20 minutes
Serves 10

Per Serving:
Calories: 527
Fat: 20.5g
Carbs: 66.3g
Fibre: 6.5g
Protein: 19.4g

- 500g fine oatmeal
- 200g plain flour
- 200g wholemeal flour
- 1 tbsp quick-action yeast
- A pinch salt
- 1 tsp baking powder
- 1 tsp baking soda
- 60g butter, warmed
- 10 rashers streaky bacon
- 200g cheddar cheese, grated

Instructions
1. In a mixing bowl, thoroughly combine the oatmeal, flour, yeast, and salt. Make a well in the centre of the mixture, then slowly and gradually add 1 litre of warm water.
2. Stir to combine well. Now, whisk in the baking powder, baking soda, and butter.
3. Spoon the batter into the prepared baking tins. Place one baking tin in each drawer.
4. Select zone 1 and pair it with "BAKE" at 180°C for 20 minutes. Select "MATCH" followed by the "START/STOP" button.
5. After 15 minutes, top your cake with bacon and cheese; reinsert drawers to resume cooking; cook until the cheese has fully melted.
6. Serve immediately and enjoy!

Classic Cottage Loaf

Prep time: 1.5 hour
Cook time: 30 minutes
Serves 10

Per Serving:
Calories: 207
Fat: 6.5g
Carbs: 31.3g
Fibre: 1.5g
Protein: 4.4g

- 240ml water warm
- 2 tsp active dry yeast
- 2 tsp granulated sugar
- 1/2 tsp salt
- 60g lard, cut into small pieces
- 400g strong plain flour

Instructions
1. Whisk the water with yeast and sugar in a mixing dish; let the mixture sit for about 10 minutes.
2. Add the flour to a large mixing bowl. Now, create a well in the centre, and gradually and slowly stir in the yeast mixture.
3. Stir in the salt and melted lard, beat again to combine well. Tip the dough onto a lightly floured work surface and continue kneading your dough until a satin-smooth dough forms.
4. Then, place your dough in a lightly oiled bowl and cover it with a cling film. Leave to rise for about 1 hour, until doubled in size.
5. Divide your dough in half and place the loaves in two lightly greased mini loaf tins. Leave to rise for about 20 minutes.
6. Select zone 1 and pair it with "BAKE" at 165°C for 30 minutes. Select "MATCH" followed by the "START/STOP" button.
7. Check your loaves for doneness and let them sit on a cooling rack for about 10 minutes before serving. Devour!

Blackpool Milk Roll

Prep time: 1.5 hour
Cook time: 30 minutes
Serves 8

Per Serving:
Calories: 297
Fat: 8.9g
Carbs: 45.7g
Fibre: 1.4g
Protein: 7.8g

- Tangzhong:
- 30g bread flour
- 160ml whole milk
- Dough:
- 120ml whole milk, cold
- 1 large egg, cold
- 350g bread flour
- 60g sugar
- 1 tsp active dry yeast
- 1/2 tsp kosher salt
- 60g butter, softened
- Egg Wash:
- 1 large egg
- 1 tablespoon water

Instructions
1. Make the tangzhong: In a small saucepan, cook the flour and milk over medium-low heat, whisking constantly, until the mixture thickens; it will take about 3 minutes.
2. Add the tangzhong to the bowl of a stand mixer fitted with a dough hook.
3. Add remaining dough ingredients. Knead the dough on medium speed for about 10 minutes.
4. Form the dough into a ball, place it into the bowl and cover it with a cling foil; let your dough rise for about 1 hour, until the dough doubles in size.
5. Lightly grease two cake tins with butter. Shape the dough into 8 balls. Transfer them to the prepared tins.
6. Make the egg wash. Lightly brush the tops of the rolls with the egg wash.
7. Select zone 1 and pair it with "BAKE" at 165°C for 30 minutes. Select "MATCH" followed by the "START/STOP" button.
8. Check your rolls for doneness and let them sit on a cooling rack for about 10 minutes before serving.

Bon appétit!

Classic Bannock

Prep time: 1.2 hour
Cook time: 10 minutes
Serves 4

Per Serving:
Calories: 53
Fat: 15.1g
Carbs: 94.3g
Fibre: 3.6g
Protein: 8.5g

- 1 tsp brown sugar
- 1 tsp sea salt
- 7g sachet fast-action yeast
- 250g strong white flour
- 70g butter, softened
- 200g raisins
- 20g golden caster sugar
- 2 tbsp milk for glazing

Instructions
1. Remove crisper plates from your Ninja Foodi. Line the zone 1 and 2 drawers with baking parchment.
2. In a mixing bowl, whisk 250ml of warm water with sugar, salt, and yeast; let it sit for about 10 minutes to activate the yeast.
3. Add the prepared yeast to the flour; add the butter, raisins, and golden caster sugar; mix to combine well. Knead the dough until smooth and satin-like dough forms.
4. After that, shape the dough into a ball and place it in the bowl. Cover and leave the dough in a warm place for about 1 hour, until doubled in size.
5. Divide the dough into 4 balls and flatten them using your hands. Lightly brush them with the milk.
6. Select zone 1 and pair it with "BAKE" at 165°C for 10 minutes. Select "MATCH" followed by the "START/STOP" button.
7. When zone 1 time reaches 5 minutes, turn the Bannock over and reinsert the drawer to continue cooking.

Bon appétit!

Grandma's Stottie Cake

Prep time: 1.5 hour
Cook time: 30 minutes
Serves 6

Per Serving:
Calories: 232
Fat: 1.1g
Carbs: 45.3g
Fibre: 1.6g
Protein: 6.6g

- 120 ml tepid water
- 7g dried yeast
- 1 tsp brown sugar
- 340g strong white flour
- 1 tsp salt
- 100ml milk, warmed

Instructions
1. Whisk the water with yeast and sugar in a mixing dish; let the mixture sit for about 10 minutes.
2. Add the flour to a large mixing bowl. Now, create a well in the centre, and gradually and slowly stir in the yeast mixture.
3. Stir in the salt and milk; beat again to combine well. Tip the dough onto a lightly floured work surface and continue kneading your dough until a satin-smooth dough forms.
4. Then, place your dough in a lightly oiled bowl and cover it with a cling film. Leave to rise for about 1 hour, until doubled in size.
5. Knock the dough down and split it into two balls. Roll them into even disks.
6. Place the disks in two lightly greased mini loaf tins. Leave to rise for about 15 minutes. Prick the tops with a fork several times.
7. Select zone 1 and pair it with "BAKE" at 165°C for 30 minutes. Select "MATCH" followed by the "START/STOP" button.

Devour!

Sausage and Coriander Pilaf

Prep time: 5 minutes
Cook time: 20 minutes
Serves 5

Per Serving:
Calories: 498
Fat: 23.1g
Carbs: 55.1g
Fibre: 3.1g
Protein: 16g

- 300g long grain rice
- 300g sausages, meat squeezed from the skins
- 1 celery stick, sliced
- 1 tbsp olive oil
- 1 large onion, sliced
- 2 garlic cloves, chopped
- 1 tsp fennel seeds
- 100g frozen peas
- 200ml hot chicken stock
- 400g can tomatoes, chopped

Instructions
1. Lightly grease two baking tins with cooking oil.
2. Cook the rice according to the pack instructions; fluff the rice with a fork and divide it between the prepared baking tins.
3. Divide the other ingredients between the prepared tins. Lower the tins into both drawers.
4. Select zone 1 and pair it with "AIR FRY" at 185°C for 20 minutes. Select "MATCH" to duplicate settings across both zones. Press the "START/STOP" button.
5. When zone 1 time reaches 10 minutes, gently stir the ingredients to ensure even cooking. Reinsert the drawers to continue cooking.

Enjoy!

CHAPTER 6
VEGETARIAN & VEGAN

Quorn and Mushroom Burgers

Prep time: 5 minutes
Cook time: 20 minutes
Serves 4

Per Serving:
Calories: 573
Fat: 29.1g
Carbs: 56.1g
Fibre: 3.1g
Protein: 20.4g

- 250g Quorn mince, frozen
- 2 medium spring onions, chopped
- 1 small red chilli, chopped
- 1 large eggs, beaten
- 1/2 tsp cumin
- 1 tsp paprika
- 1 tbsp plain flour
- 1 tbsp olive oil
- 1 tsp olive oil
- 2 cloves garlic, finely chopped
- 80g breadcrumbs
- 1 tsp mustard powder
- Sea salt and ground black pepper, to taste
- 4 soft burger buns

Instructions
1. Insert the crisper plates in both drawers and spray them with cooking oil.
2. In your blender or a food processor, thoroughly combine all the ingredients. Shape the mixture into 4 patties and spray them with nonstick cooking oil. Now, arrange them in the lightly greased drawers.
3. Select zone 1 and pair it with "AIR FRY" at 190°C for 20 minutes. Select "MATCH" to duplicate settings across both zones. Press the "START/STOP" button.
4. When zone 1 time reaches 10 minutes, turn the burgers over, spray them with cooking oil on the other side, and reinsert the drawers to continue cooking.
5. Serve warm patties in hamburger buns with toppings of choice. Serve on burger buns with iceberg lettuce, slices of tomatoes and onion to serve.

Bon appétit!

Veggie Tacos with Guacamole

Prep time: 10 minutes
Cook time: 20 minutes
Serves 4

Per Serving:
Calories: 344
Fat: 23.2g
Carbs: 33.3g
Fibre: 12.5g
Protein: 7.6g

- 500g portobello mushrooms, sliced
- 2 large bell peppers, deseeded and halved
- Sea salt and freshly ground black pepper, to taste
- 1 tsp dried Mexican oregano
- Guacamole:
- 2 medium avocados, very ripe but not bruised
- 1 medium lime, juiced
- 1 small onion, finely chopped
- 2 tbsp olive oil
- 1 tsp paprika
- 4 medium corn tortillas
- 1 medium ripe tomato
- 2 tbsp fresh coriander, leaves and stalks chopped
- 1 chilli, red or green, deseeded and finely chopped

Instructions
1. Insert crisper plates in both drawers. Spray the crisper plates with nonstick cooking oil.
2. Toss the mushrooms and peppers with olive oil and spices.
3. Place the mushrooms in the zone 1 drawer; place the peppers in the zone 2 drawer.
4. Select zone 1 and pair it with "AIR FRY" at 185°C for 13 minutes. Select zone 2 and pair it with "ROAST" at 180°C for 15 minutes. Select "SYNC" followed by the "START/STOP" button.
5. At the half point, stir your ingredients to promote even cooking. Reinsert the drawers to resume cooking.
6. In the meantime, halve and stone your avocados; add the other ingredients and roughly mash everything together with a whisk or fork. Reserve.
7. Add tortillas to both drawers. Select "REHEAT" at 170°C for 5 minutes.
8. Add the mushrooms to the warmed tortillas; top them with peppers and serve with guacamole. Enjoy!

Mushroom & Courgette Pilaf

Prep time: 10 minutes
Cook time: 20 minutes
Serves 5

Per Serving:
Calories: 329
Fat: 7.1g
Carbs: 50.5g
Fibre: 7.1g
Protein: 16.9g

- 2 tsp olive oil, melted
- 300g quinoa, soaked overnight and rinsed
- 1 litre vegetable broth
- 1 chilli pepper, sliced
- 1 medium leek, minced
- 2 garlic cloves, minced
- 200g white mushrooms, sliced
- 1 medium courgette, peeled and sliced
- 100g frozen green peas

Instructions
1. Brush the inside of two baking trays with olive oil.
2. Mix the quinoa with the other ingredients and spoon the mixture into the prepared baking trays. Add the baking trays to the drawers.
3. Select zone 1 and pair it with "BAKE" at 180°C for 20 minutes. Select "MATCH" to duplicate settings across both zones. Press the "START/STOP" button.
4. Spoon your pilaf into serving bowls and serve immediately. Enjoy!

Herb Cauliflower with Mushrooms

Prep time: 10 minutes
Cook time: 10 minutes
Serves 4

Per Serving:
Calories: 90
Fat: 2.8g
Carbs: 13.7g
Fibre: 4.1g
Protein: 6.3g

- 500g cauliflower florets
- 500g brown mushrooms, halved
- 2 tsp olive oil
- 1 tsp garlic granules
- 1 tsp dried basil
- 1 tsp dried parsley flakes
- 1 tsp dried oregano
- 1 tsp paprika
- Sea salt and ground black pepper, to taste
- A handful of fresh coriander, leaves and stalks chopped

Instructions
1. Toss the cauliflower florets and mushrooms with olive oil and spices. Add the cauliflower to the zone 1 drawer and mushrooms to the zone 2 drawer.
2. Select zone 1 and pair it with "ROAST" at 200°C for 8 minutes. Select zone 2 and pair it with "ROAST" at 180°C for 10 minutes. Select "SYNC" followed by the "START/STOP" button.
3. At the halfway point, toss your food and reinsert the drawers to resume cooking.
4. Garnish your vegetables with fresh coriander and enjoy!

Mushrooms and Cherry Tomatoes on Toast

Prep time: 5 minutes
Cook time: 10 minutes
Serves 5

Per Serving:
Calories: 427
Fat: 14.6g
Carbs: 56.9g
Fibre: 5.6g
Protein: 19.1g

- 400g button mushrooms, halved
- 200g cherry tomatoes
- 2 tbsp olive oil
- Sea salt and ground black pepper, to taste
- 1 tsp paprika
- 1 tsp garlic granules
- 1 loaf of crusty bread, sliced
- 100g parmesan cheese, grated

Instructions

1. Toss the mushrooms and cherry tomatoes with olive oil and spices. Add the mushrooms to the zone 1 drawer and cherry tomatoes to the zone 2 drawer.
2. Select zone 1 and pair it with "ROAST" at 200°C for 8 minutes. Select zone 2 and pair it with "ROAST" at 180°C for 10 minutes. Select "SYNC" followed by the "START/STOP" button.
3. At the halfway point, toss your food and reinsert the drawers to resume cooking.
4. Top bread slices with mushrooms, cherry tomatoes, and cheese. Select "REHEAT" at 170°C for 3 minutes.
5. Serve immediately and enjoy!

British-Style Gratin Dauphinois

Prep time: 5 minutes
Cook time: 30 minutes
Serves 5

Per Serving:
Calories: 367
Fat: 21.6g
Carbs: 32.4g
Fibre: 5.5g
Protein: 11.5g

- 400g Desirée potatoes, sliced to a width of 3mm
- 2 bell peppers, deseeded and sliced
- 300g tofu, crumbled
- 200ml tomato sauce
- 1 medium leek, sliced
- 2 garlic cloves, minced
- 2 tbsp fresh coriander, chopped
- 1 tbsp olive oil
- 1 tsp paprika
- Sea salt and ground black pepper, to taste
- 100ml full-fat milk
- 200ml carton double cream
- 20g parmesan, freshly grated

Instructions

1. Grease two baking trays with cooking oil.
2. Divide half the potato slices between the prepared baking trays, slightly overlapping the slices.
3. In a mixing bowl, thoroughly combine all the ingredients, except for the parmesan cheese. Divide the mixture between the prepared baking trays.
4. Finish off layering the rest of the potatoes. Lower the baking trays into the drawers (without crisper plates).
5. Select zone 1 and pair it with "BAKE" at 180°C for 30 minutes. Select "MATCH" followed by the "START/STOP" button.
6. When zone 1 time reaches 15 minutes, scatter the cheese over the top and reinsert the drawer to continue cooking.

Bon appétit!

Carrot & Oat Balls

Prep time: 5 minutes
Cook time: 15 minutes
Serves 6

Per Serving:
Calories: 300
Fat: 19.6g
Carbs: 27.8g
Fibre: 4.5g
Protein: 5.5g

- 150g old-fashioned rolled oats
- 30g raw pecans, finely chopped
- 1 tbsp flaxseed meal
- 100g cup almond butter
- 2 tbsp maple syrup
- 1/2 tsp ground cinnamon
- 1/2 tsp ground nutmeg
- 100g grated carrot
- 30g sultanas

Instructions
1. Insert the crisper plates in both drawers and spray them with cooking oil.
2. In a mixing bowl, thoroughly combine the ingredients. Shape the mixture into small balls and slightly flatten them with a fork.
3. Arrange the carrot balls in the cooking basket.
4. Select zone 1 and pair it with "AIR FRY" at 190°C for 15 minutes. Select "MATCH" to duplicate settings across both zones. Press the "START/STOP" button.
5. When zone 1 time reaches 8 minutes, turn the balls over and reinsert the drawer to continue cooking.

Bon appétit!

Vegan "Chicken" with Asparagus

Prep time: 10 minutes
Cook time: 12 minutes
Serves 4

Per Serving:
220
Fat: 3.6g
Carbs: 22.8g
Fibre: 5g
Protein: 25.5g

- 100g soy curls
- 200ml hot water
- 40g corn flour
- 40g plain flour
- 1 tbsp nutritional yeast
- 2 tsp miso paste
- 1 tsp poultry seasoning mix
- 400g asparagus, trimmed
- Sea salt and ground black pepper, to taste
- 2 tsp olive oil

Instructions
1. Insert the crisper plates in both drawers and spray them with cooking oil.
2. Soak soy curls in hot water for approximately 10 minutes. Drain the soy curls in a mesh sieve, squeezing out as much liquid as possible.
3. Combine the flour, nutritional yeast, miso paste, and poultry seasoning mix in a shallow bowl.
4. Toss asparagus with salt and pepper.
5. Roll soy curls over the dry flour mixture until they're all evenly coated. Arrange the prepared soy curls in the zone 1 drawer and asparagus in the zone 2 drawer. Brush them with oil.
6. Select zone 1 and pair it with "AIR FRY" at 200°C for 12 minutes. Select zone 2 and pair it with "ROAST" at 200°C for 8 minutes. Select "SYNC" followed by the "START/STOP" button.
7. At the halfway point, toss your food to ensure even cooking; reinsert the drawers to resume cooking. Bon appétit!

Lemony Falafel with Tahini Sauce

Prep time: 10 minutes
Cook time: 20 minutes
Serves 4

Per Serving:
Calories: 320
Fat: 16.6g
Carbs: 33.8g
Fibre: 8.5g
Protein: 11.7g

- Falafel:
- 300g canned chickpeas, drained and rinsed
- 1 large courgette, peeled
- 1 medium onion, chopped
- 2 garlic cloves, peeled
- 1 medium bell pepper, deseeded
- 1 chili pepper, deseeded
- 2 tbsp parsley, chopped
- 1 small lemon, juiced
- Sea salt and ground black pepper, to taste
- Tahini Sauce:
- 100ml tahini
- 1 tbsp apple cider vinegar
- 2 tbsp soy sauce

Instructions
1. Insert the crisper plates in both drawers and spray them with cooking oil.
2. Mix all the ingredients for the falafel in your food processor or a high-speed blender. Shape the mixture into 8 balls and lower them into both drawers.
3. Select zone 1 and pair it with "AIR FRY" at 185°C for 20 minutes. Select "MATCH" to duplicate settings across both zones. Press the "START/STOP" button.
4. When zone 1 time reaches 10 minutes, turn the falafel balls over and reinsert the drawers to continue cooking.
5. Mix the ingredients for the sauce. Serve warm falafel balls with tahini sauce on the side and enjoy!

Spiced Cabbage Steaks

Prep time: 10 minutes
Cook time: 8 minutes
Serves 2

Per Serving:
Calories: 255
Fat: 14.4g
Carbs: 31.3g
Fibre: 12.5g
Protein: 7g

- 1 medium head of green cabbage
- 2 tbsp sesame oil
- 1 tbsp hot sauce
- Sea salt and ground black pepper, to taste
- 1 tsp smoked paprika
- 1 tsp garlic powder
- 1 tsp dried basil
- 1 tsp dried rosemary

Instructions
1. On a cutting board, cut your cabbage into 6 to 7 slices.
2. Toss cabbage slices with the other ingredients.
3. Select zone 1 and pair it with "AIR FRY" at 195°C for 8 minutes. Select "MATCH" to duplicate settings across both zones. Press the "START/STOP" button.
4. When zone 1 time reaches 4 minutes, turn cabbage steaks over and reinsert the drawers to continue cooking.

Bon appétit!

Cheese Aubergine Rolls

Prep time: 10 minutes
Cook time: 8 minutes
Serves 2

Per Serving:
Calories: 186
Fat: 6.4g
Carbs: 26.5g
Fibre: 9.5g
Protein: 9.7g

- 2 medium aubergines, slice lengthways into 1/2cm-thick slices
- 2 bell peppers, deveined and cut into halves
- Sea salt and ground black pepper, to taste
- 1 tsp paprika
- 1 tsp garlic granules
- 1/2 tsp ground cumin
- 1 tbsp olive oil
- 200g cottage cheese, crumbled
- 4 sun-dried tomatoes in oil, chopped

Instructions
1. Insert the crisper plates in both drawers and spray them with cooking oil.
2. Toss aubergine slices and bell peppers with spices and olive oil. Arrange them in both drawers.
3. Select zone 1 and pair it with "ROAST" at 190°C for 12 minutes. Select "MATCH" to duplicate settings across both zones. Press the "START/STOP" button.
4. Meanwhile, mix the cheese with sun-dried tomatoes and reserve. Add chopped roasted peppers to the mixture.
5. Top the aubergine slices with the cheese/pepper mixture; roll them up and secure them with toothpicks; carefully lower the aubergine rolls into both drawers.
6. Select zone 1 and pair it with "AIR FRY" at 180°C for 5 minutes. Select "MATCH" to duplicate settings across both zones. Press the "START/STOP" button.

Bon appétit!

Herb Au Gratin Potatoes

Prep time: 5 minutes
Cook time: 30 minutes
Serves 5

Per Serving:
Calories: 555
Fat: 35.6g
Carbs: 39.4g
Fibre: 3.9g
Protein: 21.5g

- 400g Desirée potatoes, sliced to a width of 3mm
- 1 tbsp butter
- 2 bell peppers, deseeded and sliced
- 300g Gruyère cheese, shredded
- 200ml tomato sauce
- 1 tbsp rosemary, chopped
- 1 tbsp thyme, chopped
- 1 medium leek, sliced
- 2 garlic cloves, minced
- 2 tbsp fresh coriander, chopped
- 1 tbsp olive oil
- Sea salt and ground black pepper, to taste
- 100ml full-fat milk
- 200ml carton double cream
- 100g bread crumbs

Instructions
1. Slice the potatoes using a mandolin or vegetable slicer. Grease two baking trays with the melted butter.
2. Divide half the potato slices between the prepared baking trays, slightly overlapping the slices.
3. In a mixing bowl, thoroughly combine all the ingredients, except the breadcrumbs. Divide the mixture between the prepared baking trays.
4. Finish off layering the rest of the potatoes. Lower the baking trays into the drawers (without crisper plates).
5. Select zone 1 and pair it with "BAKE" at 180°C for 30 minutes. Select "MATCH" followed by the "START/STOP" button.
6. When zone 1 time reaches 15 minutes, sprinkle with the breadcrumbs and reinsert the drawer to continue cooking.
7. Test your gratin with a knife to see if it is cooked and tender throughout. Cool slightly before cutting into wedges and serving.

Bon appétit!

Za'atar Potato Latkes

Prep time: 5 minutes
Cook time: 15 minutes
Serves 4

Per Serving:
Calories: 406
Fat: 5.6g
Carbs: 78.1g
Fibre: 9g
Protein: 11.9g

- 4 large Maris Piper potatoes, scrubbed
- 1 onion, peeled and chopped
- 1 garlic clove, minced
- 2 medium eggs, beaten
- 4 tbsp plain flour
- 1 tbsp za'atar
- Sea salt and ground black pepper, to taste
- 1 tbsp olive oil

Instructions
1. Insert crisper plates in both drawers. Spray the crisper plates with nonstick cooking oil.
2. Coarsely grate your potatoes with skin. Now, wring out the liquid with a clean tea towel.
3. Add the other ingredients to the grated potatoes. Shape the mixture into latkes, flattening gently with a wide spatula.
4. Arrange potato latkes in your cooking basket.
5. Select zone 1 and pair it with "AIR FRY" at 180°C for 15 minutes. Select "MATCH" followed by the "START/STOP" button. Flip potato latkes halfway through the cooking time.
6. Bon appétit!

Mixed Air Fryer Vegetables

Prep time: 5 minutes
Cook time: 15 minutes
Serves 4

Per Serving:
Calories: 106
Fat: 3.6g
Carbs: 15.9g
Fibre: 5.5g
Protein: 3.5g

- 200g Brussels sprouts, halved
- 400g red beetroot, peeled and diced
- 2 carrots, deseeded and quartered
- 1 tbsp olive oil
- 1 tsp paprika
- Sea salt and ground black pepper, to taste

Instructions
1. Grease two baking trays with cooking oil.
2. Toss your vegetables with olive oil, paprika, salt, and black pepper.
3. Select zone 1 and pair it with "ROAST" at 200°C for 10 minutes. Select zone 2 and pair it with "ROAST" at 190°C for 15 minutes. Select "SYNC" followed by the "START/STOP" button.
4. At the half point, turn your ingredients over to promote even cooking. Reinsert drawers to resume cooking.

Bon appétit!

CHAPTER 7
APPETIZERS & SNACKS

Curried Corn on the Cob

Prep time: 5 minutes
Cook time: 15 minutes
Serves 4

Per Serving:
Calories: 236
Fat: 11.6g
Carbs: 30.8g
Fibre: 3.5g
Protein: 7.3g

- 4 ears corn on the cob, halved
- 40g butter, room temperature
- 40g parmesan cheese, grated
- 1 tbsp curry paste
- Flaky sea salt and ground black pepper, to taste

Instructions
1. In a small mixing bowl, thoroughly combine the butter, parmesan cheese, curry paste, sea salt, and black pepper. Cut 8 pieces of tin foil and place 1/2 of the cob on each piece.
2. Transfer the packets to the cooking basket.
3. Select zone 1 and pair it with "BAKE" at 190°C for 15 minutes. Select "MATCH" followed by the "START/STOP" button.
4. At the halfway point, toss the cooking basket and reinsert the drawer to continue cooking.
5. Serve warm and enjoy!

Sweet Potato Chips

Prep time: 5 minutes
Cook time: 25 minutes
Serves 4

Per Serving:
Calories: 184
Fat: 3.6g
Carbs: 35g
Fibre: 4.4g
Protein: 4.1g

- 800g sweet potatoes, hand-cut chips, thick
- 1 tbsp olive oil
- 1 tbsp dried basil
- 1 tbsp dried parsley flakes
- 1 tsp chilli flakes

Instructions
1. Insert crisper plates in both drawers. Spray the crisper plates with nonstick cooking oil.
2. Select zone 1 and pair it with "AIR FRY" at 190°C for 25 minutes. Select "MATCH" followed by the "START/STOP" button.
3. At the halfway point, gently stir the ingredients using a wooden spoon; reinsert the drawers to resume cooking.
Enjoy!

Classic British Faggots

Prep time: 5 minutes
Cook time: 20 minutes
Serves 6

Per Serving:
Calories: 488
Fat: 32g
Carbs: 20.9g
Fibre: 2.1g
Protein: 29.1g

- 400g pack pork shoulder, diced
- 400g pig liver
- 180g pack sage & onion stuffing mix
- 1 tbsp olive oil

Instructions
1. In a mixing bowl, thoroughly combine all the ingredients for the faggots. Mould the mixture into equal balls.
2. Select zone 1 and pair it with "AIR FRY" at 185°C for 20 minutes. Select "MATCH" to duplicate settings across both zones. Press the "START/STOP" button.
3. At the halfway point, turn the faggots over and reinsert the drawers to resume cooking.
4. Serve meatballs with cocktail sticks.

Bon appétit!

Parmesan Okra Chips

Prep time: 5 minutes
Cook time: 20 minutes
Serves 5

Per Serving:
Calories: 252
Fat: 7.9g
Carbs: 32.1g
Fibre: 7.2g
Protein: 12.1g

- 1kg okra, cut into halves lengthwise
- 1 tbsp olive oil
- 1 tsp onion powder
- 1 tsp garlic granules
- 1 tsp turmeric powder
- Sea salt and ground black pepper, to taste
- 100g breadcrumbs
- 100g parmesan cheese, grated

Instructions
1. Toss okra halves with olive oil, spices, and breadcrumbs until they are well coated on all sides.
2. Add okra to both drawers of your Ninja Foodi (with a crisper plate inserted).
3. Select zone 1 and pair it with "AIR FRY" at 180°C for 20 minutes. Select "MATCH" followed by the "START/STOP" button.
4. At the halfway point, shake the drawers to ensure even cooking; add cheese and reinsert the drawers to resume cooking. Bon appétit!

Easy Cheesy Brussels Sprouts

Prep time: 5 minutes
Cook time: 20 minutes
Serves 5

Per Serving:
Calories: 272
Fat: 11.2g
Carbs: 31g
Fibre: 8.5g
Protein: 15.1g

- 1kg Brussels sprouts, cut into halves
- 1 tbsp olive oil
- 1 tsp dried parsley flakes
- 1 tsp onion powder
- 1 tsp garlic granules
- Sea salt and ground black pepper, to taste
- 80g breadcrumbs
- 100g goat cheese, grated

Instructions
1. Toss Brussels sprouts with olive oil, spices, and breadcrumbs until they are well coated on all sides.
2. Add Brussels sprouts to both drawers of your Ninja Foodi (with a crisper plate inserted).
3. Select zone 1 and pair it with "AIR FRY" at 180°C for 20 minutes. Select "MATCH" followed by the "START/STOP" button.
4. At the halfway point, shake the drawers to ensure even cooking; add cheese and reinsert the drawers to resume cooking.

Bon appétit!

Baked Spinach Dip

Prep time: 5 minutes
Cook time: 15 minutes
Serves 9

Per Serving:
Calories: 170
Fat: 13g
Carbs: 4.3g
Fibre: 0.8g
Protein: 7.1g

- 200ml soured cream
- 2 x 200g packs feta cheese, crumbled
- 3 tbsp sliced jalapeno chilli
- 2 handfuls of baby spinach
- A small handful of coriander leaves, chopped

Instructions
1. Mix all ingredients in a bowl; then, spoon the mixture into a lightly buttered casserole dish.
2. Select zone 1 and pair it with "BAKE" at 170°C for 15 minutes. Select "MATCH" followed by the "START/STOP" button.
3. Serve warm dip with chips or vegetable sticks for dipping.

Bon appétit!

Sriracha Golden Cauliflower

Prep time: 10 minutes
Cook time: 20 minutes
Serves 5

Per Serving:
Calories: 107
Fat: 3.3g
Carbs: 17.3g
Fibre: 4.1g
Protein: 3.9g

- 1kg cauliflower florets
- 50ml Sriracha sauce
- 2 tbsp golden syrup
- 1 tbsp olive oil
- Sea salt and ground black pepper, to taste

Instructions
1. Insert the crisper plates in both drawers and spray them with cooking oil.
2. Toss the cauliflower florets with the other ingredients. Arrange the cauliflower florets on the prepared crisper plates.
3. Select zone 1 and pair it with "ROAST" at 190°C for 20 minutes. Select "MATCH" to duplicate settings across both zones. Press the "START/STOP" button.

Bon appétit!

Summer Squash Wedges

Prep time: 10 minutes
Cook time: 25 minutes
Serves 5

Per Serving:
Calories: 70
Fat: 1.3g
Carbs: 7.3g
Fibre: 2.4g
Protein: 2.6g

- 1kg summer squash, cut into wedges
- 1 tsp cayenne pepper
- Sea salt and ground black pepper, to taste
- 1 tsp coconut oil

Instructions
1. Insert crisper plates in both drawers. Spray the crisper plates with nonstick cooking oil.
2. Brush summer squash with spices and coconut oil; arrange them in both drawers.
3. Select zone 1 and pair it with "ROAST" at 200°C for 25 minutes. Select "MATCH" followed by the "START/STOP" button.
4. Turn over summer squash wedges halfway through the cooking time to ensure even cooking.

Bon appétit!

Squash Beignets

Prep time: 10 minutes
Cook time: 18 minutes
Serves 5

Per Serving:
Calories: 177
Fat: 3.3g
Carbs: 31.9g
Fibre: 2.6g
Protein: 4.6g

- 1 small butternut squash, grated
- 100g plain flour
- 50g corn flour
- 1 tsp baking powder
- 1 medium eggs, beaten
- 2 tsp olive oil

Instructions
1. Mix all the ingredients in a bowl, except the oil.
2. Add the batter to a piping bag fitted with an open star tip. Pipe your beignets onto two lightly greased baking trays. Brush them with nonstick oil.
3. Select zone 1 and pair it with "BAKE" at 180°C for 18 minutes. Select "MATCH" followed by the "START/STOP" button.

Bon appétit!

Worcestershire Chicken Wings

Prep time: 10 minutes
Cook time: 25 minutes
Serves 6

Per Serving:
Calories: 244
Fat: 17.5g
Carbs: 1.8g
Fibre: 0.2g
Protein: 18.7g

- 600g chicken wings, drumettes & flats
- 1 tbsp Worcestershire sauce
- 1 tbsp olive oil
- 1 tbsp corn flour
- 1 tsp garlic granules
- 1 tsp cayenne pepper
- Sea salt and ground black pepper, to taste

Instructions
1. Insert crisper plates in both drawers. Spray the crisper plates with nonstick cooking oil.
2. Toss chicken wings with the other ingredients. Add the chicken to the cooking basket.
3. Select zone 1 and pair it with "ROAST" at 200°C for 25 minutes. Select "MATCH" followed by the "START/STOP" button.
4. Turn over summer squash wedges halfway through the cooking time to ensure even cooking.
5. Cook until the tops of the wings are starting to char a little.

Bon appétit!

Colourful Vegetable Skewers

Prep time: 5 minutes
Cook time: 18 minutes
Serves 4

Per Serving:
Calories: 167
Fat: 4g
Carbs: 31.7g
Fibre: 8.2g
Protein: 4.8g

- 2 medium shallots, quartered
- 4 bell peppers, deseeded and sliced
- 1 medium aubergine, sliced
- 200g cherry tomatoes
- Sea salt and ground black pepper, to taste
- 1 tsp paprika
- 1 tbsp olive oil
- 1 tsp balsamic vinegar
- 1 tbsp maple syrup

Instructions
1. Toss all the ingredients until vegetables are well coated on all sides.
2. Alternately thread the vegetables onto the skewers until you run out of the ingredients.
3. Then, add the vegetables to the zone 1 and 2 drawers.
4. Select zone 1 and pair it with "ROAST" at 180°C for 18 minutes. Select "MATCH" followed by the "START/STOP" button.
5. At the halfway point, turn the skewers over and reinsert the drawers to resume cooking.

Bon appétit!

CHAPTER 8
DESSERTS

Bakewell Tart

Prep time: 10 minutes
Cook time: 33 minutes
Serves 8

Per Serving:
Calories: 315
Fat: 14g
Carbs: 44.6g
Fibre: 1.3g
Protein: 4.3g

- 100g butter, softened
- 1 large egg
- 150g golden caster sugar
- 1/2 tsp anise star, ground
- 1 vanilla pod, split lengthways and seeds scraped out
- 180g self-raising flour
- 1/2 tsp baking powder
- 100g raspberry jam
- 40g almonds, slivered

Instructions
1. Lightly grease two baking trays with nonstick cooking oil.
2. Beat the butter and egg until pale and frothy. Then, add the sugar, anise, and vanilla, and mix to combine well.
3. Stir in the flour and baking powder; mix again to combine well. Divide the batter between the prepared tins.
4. Select zone 1 and pair it with "BAKE" at 160°C for 25 minutes. Select "MATCH" followed by the "START/STOP" button.
5. Spread the raspberry jam evenly on the cooled crust. Sprinkle the almonds evenly on top.
6. Bake your tart at 160°C for a further 8 minutes.

Bon appétit!

Peach & Chocolate Galette

Prep time: 10 minutes
Cook time: 30 minutes
Serves 9

Per Serving:
Calories: 395
Fat: 25.4g
Carbs: 37.6g
Fibre: 2.8g
Protein: 5g

- 250g plain flour, plus more to dust
- 200g cold butter, diced
- 65g light brown soft sugar
- 2 eggs, 1 yolk only, 1 whole egg beaten to glaze
- 2 small peaches, stoned and sliced
- 130g dark chocolate, melted

Instructions
1. Lightly grease two baking trays with nonstick cooking oil.
2. Mix the dry ingredients in a bowl. Then, in a separate bowl, mix the liquid ingredients.
3. Add the dry mixture to the liquid ingredients; mix again to combine well. Divide the pastry into two balls.
4. Roll each pastry out in between two pieces of baking parchment to a large disc. Add them to the prepared baking trays.
5. Top them with peaches and fold in the edges of the pastry to slightly overlap the fruit.
6. Select zone 1 and pair it with "BAKE" at 170°C for 30 minutes. Select "MATCH" followed by the "START/STOP" button.
7. Sprinkle with melted chocolate and leave to cool to room temperature.

Bon appétit!

Chocolate Brownie Cake

Prep time: 12 minutes
Cook time: 20 minutes
Serves 10

Per Serving:
Calories: 365
Fat: 23.5g
Carbs: 32.6g
Fibre: 4.2g
Protein: 6.3g

- 200g dark chocolate (70-85% cacao solids), cut into chunks
- 150g unsalted butter, room temperature
- 150g brown sugar
- 2 large eggs, lightly beaten
- 100g oat flour
- 100g almond flour
- 1/4 tsp grated nutmeg
- 1 tsp ground cinnamon
- 1 tsp pure vanilla paste
- 1/2 tsp ground cloves

Instructions
1. Grease two baking tins with cooking oil.
2. Melt the chocolate, butter and sugar in your microwave. (You can also use a small saucepan and melt the ingredients at low temperature for about 2 minutes; keep a close eye on it).
3. Fold in the eggs and beat again to combine well. Stir in the other ingredients and mix until everything is well combined.
4. Select zone 1 and pair it with "BAKE" at 170°C for 20 minutes. Select "MATCH" followed by the "START/STOP" button.
5. Leave to cool to room temperature. Devour!

Chocolate Doughnuts

Prep time: 10 minutes
Cook time: 18 minutes
Serves 12

Per Serving:
Calories: 308
Fat: 15.8g
Carbs: 34.2g
Fibre: 1.9g
Protein: 5.7g

- 160g golden caster sugar
- 200g plain flour
- 1 tsp bicarbonate of soda
- 120ml natural yoghurt
- 2 small eggs, beaten
- A pinch of ground cloves
- A pinch of ground cinnamon
- 1 tsp vanilla extract
- 140g butter, melted, plus extra for greasing
- 12 tsp chocolate spread

Instructions
1. Lightly grease 12 small muffin cases with cooking oil.
2. Mix the dry ingredients in a bowl. Then, in a separate bowl, mix the liquid ingredients.
3. Add the dry mixture to the liquid ingredients; mix again to combine well.
4. Divide two-thirds of the mixture between the muffin cases. Carefully add 1 tsp chocolate spread into the centre of each; cover with the remaining mixture.
5. Select zone 1 and pair it with "BAKE" at 190°C for 18 minutes. Select "MATCH" followed by the "START/STOP" button.
6. Bake until golden and springy to the touch. Devour!

Bread and Butter Pudding

Prep time: 30 minutes
Cook time: 20 minutes
Serves 6

Per Serving:
Calories: 328
Fat: 16g
Carbs: 37.3g
Fibre: 4.1g
Protein: 10.6g

- 9 thin bread slices, cubed
- 1 large egg, beaten
- 2 tbsp butter
- 150ml almond milk
- 150ml double cream
- 80g golden syrup
- 1/2 tsp grated nutmeg
- 1/2 tsp cinnamon powder
- 1 tsp vanilla extract
- A pinch of sea salt
- 100g almonds, slivered

Instructions
1. Place all the ingredients in a mixing bowl; stir to completely break up the bread and combine everything well; let it stand for about 30 minutes, pressing slightly with a large spatula.
2. Spoon the mixture into two lightly greased baking tins.
3. Select zone 1 and pair it with "ROAST" at 180°C for 20 minutes. Select "MATCH" to duplicate settings across both zones. Press the "START/STOP" button.

Bon appétit!

Simple Scottish Cranachan

Prep time: 10 minutes
Cook time: 5 minutes
Serves 4

Per Serving:
Calories: 415
Fat: 22.2g
Carbs: 49.7g
Fibre: 9.2g
Protein: 7.6g

- 100g oats
- 400g fresh British raspberries
- 400ml double cream
- 4 tbsp heather honey
- 2 tbsp whisky

Instructions
1. Divide the oats between two roasting tins. Place the roasting tins in the cooking baskets.
2. Select zone 1 and pair it with "BAKE" at 180°C for 5 minutes. Select "MATCH" followed by the "START/STOP" button.
3. When zone 1 time reaches 3 minutes, stir the oats and reinsert the drawers to continue cooking.
4. Whip the cream and add whisky to taste. Crush the raspberries with a fork, then ripple through the cream.
5. Divide the mixture between 4 serving glasses; add the oats, honey, and whiskey. Enjoy!

Dorset Apple Cake

Prep time: 10 minutes
Cook time: 30 minutes
Serves 8

Per Serving:
Calories: 316
Fat: 9.8g
Carbs: 53.1g
Fibre: 2.9g
Protein: 5.3g

- 230g self-raising flour
- 120g unsalted butter, diced and chilled, plus extra for the tin
- 2 tsp ground cinnamon
- 120g light brown sugar
- 1 large egg, beaten
- 9 tbsp milk
- 2 Granny Smith apples, peeled, cored and diced
- 100g raisins

Instructions
1. Lightly grease two baking trays with nonstick cooking oil.
2. Mix the dry ingredients in a bowl. Then, in a separate bowl, mix the liquid ingredients.
3. Add the dry mixture to the liquid ingredients; mix again to combine well. Fold in the apples and raisins.
4. Divide the batter between the prepared baking trays.
5. Select zone 1 and pair it with "BAKE" at 170°C for 30 minutes. Select "MATCH" followed by the "START/STOP" button.

Bon appétit!

Peach & Pistachio Frangipane

Prep time: 10 minutes
Cook time: 30 minutes
Serves 12

Per Serving:
Calories: 335
Fat: 16g
Carbs: 44.5g
Fibre: 2.9g
Protein: 5.9g

- 100g unsalted butter, melted, plus a little extra for the tin
- 200g light muscovado sugar
- 120g plain flour
- 50g pistachios, roughly chopped
- 2 tbsp milk
- 1 large egg
- 6 large ripe peaches, halved and stoned
- Frangipane:
- 100g golden caster sugar
- 100g unsalted butter, softened
- 1 egg
- 100g pistachios, ground to crumbs

Instructions
1. Lightly grease two baking tins with nonstick cooking oil.
2. Mix the dry ingredients for the batter in a bowl. Then, in a separate bowl, mix the liquid ingredients.
3. Mix the ingredients for the frangipane.
4. Add the dry mixture to the liquid ingredients; mix again to combine well.
5. Divide two-thirds of the batter between baking tins and smooth with the back of a spoon.
6. Dot the frangipane around the batter; add peaches and top with the remaining spoonfuls of batter.
7. Select zone 1 and pair it with "BAKE" at 170°C for 30 minutes. Select "MATCH" followed by the "START/STOP" button. Bake until a skewer comes out with some crumbs that are a little moist, but not raw.
8. Cool completely in the tin before cutting into squares.

The Dirty Dozen and Clean Fifteen

The Environmental Working Group (EWG) is a nonprofit, nonpartisan organization dedicated to protecting human health and the environment Its mission is to empower people to live healthier lives in a healthier environment. This organization publishes an annual list of the twelve kinds of produce, in sequence, that have the highest amount of pesticide residue-the Dirty Dozen-as well as a list of the fifteen kinds of produce that have the least amount of pesticide residue-the Clean Fifteen.

THE DIRTY DOZEN

- The 2016 Dirty Dozen includes the following produce. These are considered among the year's most important produce to buy organic:

Strawberries	Spinach
Apples	Tomatoes
Nectarines	Bell peppers
Peaches	Cherry tomatoes
Celery	Cucumbers
Grapes	Kale/collard greens
Cherries	Hot peppers

- The Dirty Dozen list contains two additional itemskale/collard greens and hot peppers-because they tend to contain trace levels of highly hazardous pesticides.

THE CLEAN FIFTEEN

- The least critical to buy organically are the Clean Fifteen list. The following are on the 2016 list:

Avocados	Papayas
Corn	Kiw
Pineapples	Eggplant
Cabbage	Honeydew
Sweet peas	Grapefruit
Onions	Cantaloupe
Asparagus	Cauliflower
Mangos	

- Some of the sweet corn sold in the United States are made from genetically engineered (GE) seedstock. Buy organic varieties of these crops to avoid GE produce.

MEASUREMENT CONVERSION CHART

VOLUME EQUIVALENTS(DRY)

US STANDARD	METRIC (APPROXIMATE)
1/8 teaspoon	0.5 mL
1/4 teaspoon	1 mL
1/2 teaspoon	2 mL
3/4 teaspoon	4 mL
1 teaspoon	5 mL
1 tablespoon	15 mL
1/4 cup	59 mL
1/2 cup	118 mL
3/4 cup	177 mL
1 cup	235 mL
2 cups	475 mL
3 cups	700 mL
4 cups	1 L

VOLUME EQUIVALENTS(LIQUID)

US STANDARD	US STANDARD (OUNCES)	METRIC (APPROXIMATE)
2 tablespoons	1 fl.oz.	30 mL
1/4 cup	2 fl.oz.	60 mL
1/2 cup	4 fl.oz.	120 mL
1 cup	8 fl.oz.	240 mL
1 1/2 cup	12 fl.oz.	355 mL
2 cups or 1 pint	16 fl.oz.	475 mL
4 cups or 1 quart	32 fl.oz.	1 L
1 gallon	128 fl.oz.	4 L

TEMPERATURES EQUIVALENTS

FAHRENHEIT(F)	CELSIUS(C) (APPROXIMATE)
225 °F	107 °C
250 °F	120 °C
275 °F	135 °C
300 °F	150 °C
325 °F	160 °C
350 °F	180 °C
375 °F	190 °C
400 °F	205 °C
425 °F	220 °C
450 °F	235 °C
475 °F	245 °C
500 °F	260 °C

WEIGHT EQUIVALENTS

US STANDARD	METRIC (APPROXIMATE)
1 ounce	28 g
2 ounces	57 g
5 ounces	142 g
10 ounces	284 g
15 ounces	425 g
16 ounces (1 pound)	455 g
1.5 pounds	680 g
2 pounds	907 g